START IT UP

Luke Johnson is one of Britain's most successful entrepreneurs, with an estimated personal fortune of £120 million. He is Chairman of Risk Capital Partners and the Royal Society of Arts, and a former Chairman of Channel 4 Television. He writes columns for the *Financial Times* and *Management Today*. In the 1990s he was Chairman of PizzaExpress, which he grew from twelve restaurants to over 250; he also founded the Strada pizzeria chain and owns Giraffe and Patisserie Valerie. He lives in London and is married with three children.

www.LukeJohnson.org

START IT UP

IT UP

Why Running Your
Own Business is Easier
Than You Think

Luke Johnson

PORTFOLIO
PENGUIN

PORTFOLIO PENGUIN

Published by the Penguin Group
Penguin Books Ltd, 80 Strand, London WC2R ORL, England
Penguin Group (USA) Inc., 375 Hudson Street, New York, New York 10014, USA
Penguin Group (Canada), 90 Eglinton Avenue East, Suite 700, Toronto, Ontario, Canada M4P 2Y3
(a division of Pearson Penguin Canada Inc.)
Penguin Ireland, 25 St Stephen's Green, Dublin 2, Ireland (a division of Penguin Books Ltd)
Penguin Group (Australia), 250 Camberwell Road,
Camberwell, Victoria 3124, Australia (a division of Pearson Australia Group Pty Ltd)
Penguin Books India Pvt Ltd, 11 Community Centre,
Panchsheel Park, New Delhi – 110 017, India
Penguin Group (NZ), 67 Apollo Drive, Rosedale, Auckland 0632, New Zealand
(a division of Pearson New Zealand Ltd)
Penguin Books (South Africa) (Pty) Ltd, 24 Sturdee Avenue,
Rosebank, Johannesburg 2196, South Africa

Penguin Books Ltd, Registered Offices: 80 Strand, London WC2R ORL, England

www.penguin.com

First published 2011
1

Copyright © Luke Johnson, 2011

The moral right of the author has been asserted

Set in 12.075/16.18 pt Sabon LT Std and Berthold Akzidenz Grotesk
Typeset by Andrew Barker Information Design
Printed in Great Britain by Clays Ltd, St Ives plc

A CIP catalogue record for this book is available from the British Library

ISBN: 978-0-670-91941-3

To Daisy, Felix and Ralph
– certainly my best ever start-ups

'All men's gains are the fruit of venturing'

Herodotus

Contents

Preface

This book is aimed at anyone who has ever thought about starting or buying a business. It is for one-man bands, as well as those who are running big companies. It is for all the dreamers who want to control their own destiny and make some money – perhaps a lot – while they're at it.

This is not a comprehensive manual, like a school textbook. It has practical advice, but what I really want the book to do is to inspire you to go out and create a new enterprise. The possibilities are endless. Whenever I meet someone who runs their own company, or read the biography of an entrepreneur, I am fascinated by the haphazard way in which they ended up being their own boss. The journey is rarely planned: it is not a career with a structure and sets of qualifications, like medicine or architecture.

Rather, entrepreneurs create their own career path by providing something new that customers will buy – at a profit. Sometimes that product or service is genuinely innovative – but often it is a conventional offering yet delivered better, cheaper or in a different place.

Some are happy to be simple freelancers and avoid the burden of employing staff. Others are more ambitious and want to build a major concern. Whoever they are, the journey they have chosen is unlikely to be the easy path – but for many it will offer much more excitement and satisfaction than the drudgery of working for others.

I think entrepreneurs are the unsung heroes of our time. They generate the jobs and taxes that keep our society civilized. They risk going broke, or maybe just working one hundred hours a week and earning very little. They battle through recessions, regulation and competition to satisfy our wants. I salute their efforts, ingenuity and commitment. This book is dedicated to them: because without dynamism and bold thinking, we would all be immeasurably poorer. I hope one or two of these chapters help motivate and provide a little guidance to the warrior entrepreneurs of our time.

Part 1
BEGINNINGS

A few failures first

Let me start with a few small, frothy matters such as failure, ambition, money, happiness and success.

The older I get, the more I ponder the true meaning of those words, and the harder I find it to define them.

Let's start with 'failure'. Now, I much prefer the word 'setback'. It has a more positive ring to it. But whatever you call it, I've had my fair share of business failures. Anyone who tells you they've never made any mistakes or had any losers is either lying, in denial, or headed for a really big fall.

Most entrepreneurs prefer to talk about their winners. That is natural and healthy: probably all entrepreneurs are ultimately optimistic and believe in a brighter future.

But in a curious way the most useful examples in life come from the things that don't work. That is how you learn to handle the pitfalls; by recovering from disaster you become more resilient and ideally better prepared for the next time.

So for a change, I thought I'd start this how-to business book with the odd how-not-to and a few please-don'ts. What follows are a handful of the most painful commercial lessons I've learned over the last two decades in the trenches.

These are some – but sadly not all – of the business mistakes I've made. To save blushes and possible legal actions I won't reveal the names of all the companies concerned, but they all happened and they were all expensive – for me, anyhow.

One of the early ones was a showbiz company. It was a catalogue of errors. I believed the published accounts, but unfortunately the books were cooked: the profits and assets were overstated and the liabilities understated. The audit partner served as a non-executive director – perhaps that had something to do with it. Worse, I didn't realize the company depended heavily on a tiny number of customers, one of whom soon took their business elsewhere.

I had invested just ahead of a recession. I thought the business was sound. But economic cycles are much bigger than any business or industry.

Just as we all think we're brilliant in a boom, everyone gets done over in a bust. It's only a question of degree.

Another less than wonderful experience was an automotive business. It was essentially a one-product company, but we installed a chief executive from a vastly larger concern. Bad move.

He expected secretaries, company cars, operating officers, first-class travel and all the rest. What he didn't do was actually run the business. He had risen so far he forgot how to do things like close a sale, read a balance sheet or negotiate with suppliers.

A third miserable time was my involvement in a construction company. I failed to notice the chief executive was having a slow-motion breakdown thanks to his wife's alcoholism.

He hid invoices in drawers and turned a blind eye to subordinates who were committing widespread fraud. All pretty grim for a high-volume, low-margin game like the building trade.

And then there was the restaurant abroad.

America remains a wonderful place for a British restaurateur to lose large sums of money. I did my bit in New York a few years ago. I had the foolish idea of opening a branch of our Belgian food chain Belgo there.

Our restaurant looked fantastic, the food and service were excellent, but the project was doomed from the start. As a bad omen, Manhattan union chiefs installed a giant inflatable rat outside the construction site before we opened – for using non-union labour to build the place. We misjudged US costs, tastes, pricing and staff.

We also misjudged the finances of our joint venture partner, who promptly went broke. We fatally underestimated just how competitive the restaurant business is in other countries, and were amazed at how much lower expected restaurant returns are in the USA compared to the UK.

Altogether a sobering and expensive experience, despite all the strong Belgian beer we sold.

In the early 1990s I helped a couple of young entrepreneurs buy an oven-making business called Pavailler in Valence, France, for a symbolic one franc. It was a substantial enterprise but was losing 10 per cent on turnover for its then owner, APV.

We proposed a significant downsizing to make the operation profitable. But when the plans were presented to the local union boss and mayor, it was made clear that we would be arrested and thrown in jail if we attempted such a monstrous course of action.

Sadly, none of these particular stories has a happy

ending. Nevertheless I survived all the balls-ups and I'm still plugging away.

No doubt there will be further disappointments, but I'd like to think my average has improved over the years. It certainly ought to have. I guess my attitude has been that to make progress you constantly have to experiment, otherwise you may never find what works.

In these safety-first, risk-averse times, it can seem as if the downsides of a flop are always worse than the advantages of a winner. But that attitude leads to stagnation, particularly for the budding entrepreneur, who can always take the softer option of staying in the day job. And I am not alone in having my share of losers – all risk takers have experienced problems of one sort or another.

Frank Mars, the founder of the eponymous confectionery company – now one of the largest private corporations in the world – went bankrupt not once but twice before hitting on the formula for the Mars bar.

John Nash, the great architect responsible for building Regent Street and the Brighton Pavilion among many other glorious works, went bust fifteen years before achieving success. With talent and persistence, his genius was eventually recognized. His buildings and parks stand as permanent monuments to his ability to pick himself up and start all over again.

Richard Branson tells the story of how in the early days his Virgin Atlantic airline got into problems, and he arrived home one Saturday morning to find the Coutts Bank manager on his doorstep demanding that Virgin's entire overdraft be immediately repaid

'Give me the fruitful error any time, full of seeds, bursting with its own corrections. You can keep your sterile truth for yourself'

Vilfredo Pareto

– which could have forced his business to cease trading. Branson worked the phones for the next twenty-four hours and repaid the bank on Monday morning.

Similarly, early in his career as a manufacturer of drugs in France, one Thursday Jimmy Goldsmith faced the certainty of receivership for his fledgling commercial empire the following day. But luckily for him – remember, this was Paris – there was a bank strike the next day, so no one called in his loans, and he was able to use the time to scrape together enough money to survive and eventually become a billionaire, like Branson.

The key is to respond creatively to defeat and never give in to discouragement. Giving up is the ultimate tragedy. You need to rise every time you fall and work harder. Today's disaster soon fades and new possibilities present themselves.

I really believe that. I emphasize it now because in writing this book I am encouraging readers to go down a path that, for some, will result in something that looks a lot like failure – but the only failure is never to try, and no setback need be for ever.

It's likely there are more failures to come for me, so one ought to ask why entrepreneurs put themselves through it. The answer lies partly in boundless ambition.

Ambition – the stuff of life

Thomas Dunn English, a nineteenth-century US Democrat, said that ambition is the germ from which all nobleness proceeds. That may be so, but I think it can be a curse, rather than a privilege. Someone who is driven in work and life has a monkey on their back, always pushing them to try harder, climb higher, do better. There is no rest.

Ambition is the competitive urge that has existed from time immemorial. It is the spirit that has fuelled every great endeavour of mankind – huge constructions, marvellous inventions, stunning works of art, incredible civilizations. But the ambitious are relentless in their quest for new challenges, new things to conquer. It does not make for a quiet or relaxed life. I suspect the enterprising types are just not easily satisfied.

I don't think you can choose your fate as regards ambition. If your genes and your background are such that you have fire in your belly and a burning desire to achieve – to be an entrepreneur – then there is little to be done. Like a poet, you must give in to the siren call of the muse. You may control your destiny through your career, but you cannot deny your personality.

Lofty concepts like work–life balance may appeal to some. Going home at 4.30 p.m., spurning promotion and responsibility, early retirement – these things suit some people. But they don't suit the intended reader of this book. If you are spurred by hunger to master a task, then you will have no choice but to press on to victory, perhaps at any cost.

'Ambition is a lust that is never quenched, but grows more inflamed and madder by enjoyment'

Thomas Otway

You might ask: ambitious for what? Do entrepreneurs strive merely for success, be it material, personal or social?

Entrepreneurs certainly talk about their successes all the time, so I'm not going to bore you with that stuff about the bank balance. In my opinion true success is rather more profound than the popular notion of achievement, and harder to achieve. Beyond a certain point, the trappings of wealth are merely a game to keep boredom at bay.

For me, success is about being vitally engaged in something worthwhile, making a difference for the better, and having fun while I'm at it. It is about being a producer rather than a consumer. It is about being utterly absorbed by the task – by the struggle, even. If you are fully preoccupied by your entrepreneurial venture, consider it a partial success regardless of the final outcome.

Most straightforward business magnates are soon forgotten and their ephemeral achievements broken up, their estates squabbled over. Those who achieve lasting success remember to volunteer, remember philanthropy, remember to create things, remember decency and balance and remember to remain captains of their souls.

All of this is much easier said than done but, whether one is materially successful or not, I know that the entrepreneurial life beats the drudgery of the rat race.

Stop making excuses and get started

In my travels, I meet quite a few would-be entrepreneurs. Some of these characters have a vision of starting or buying a business, but always seem to find reasons to do nothing. Their excuses sound convincing, but in truth none of them really stands up to close examination.

First on the list tends to be a lack of capital. There are lots of solutions to this one.

My first business, when I was eighteen, was a venture with an Oxford nightclub where student friends and I promoted themed evenings and took the door money, while the venue owners kept the bar takings. The operation needed no capital at all – always the best type for absolute beginners.

Other situations may need some funding, but often less than founders think. I am often impressed at how first-time restaurateurs seem to fit out premises on a shoestring – using second-hand equipment, personally helping out with the refurbishment and so on.

Most things can be done on a budget if your life's dream depends on it.

And there is equity backing out there: if professional investors won't give it to you, there are all sorts of pockets of institutional and private cash for a sound project, from government agencies to angel investors.

It has never been easy to tap these sources of finance, so you need to be good – and persistent.

Howard Schultz, founder of Starbucks, did more than 240 presentations to raise the early-stage funding to really kick-start his coffee-bar chain.

A second imagined obstacle is income: people get addicted to a nice safe salary as an employee, and are unwilling to give it up for the uncertainties of the entrepreneurial life. It is true that plenty of the self-employed earn less than they would working for others – and may put in longer hours. But they do it because of the freedom and fulfilment it brings – and because they refuse to give up on their hopes.

During my early twenties I took little time off – when I wasn't working for others, I ran sideline businesses at weekends and during holidays – until finally I felt able to break free and become a full-time entrepreneur. In some ways I wished I had not delayed, but had taken the plunge straight from university.

I accept that there are those who have heavy domestic responsibilities – a mortgage, family obligations and so forth. But anything really worth having requires sacrifice. The alternative is to let opportunities slip by and live a life of regrets.

A third excuse is the idea: too many wannabe entrepreneurs are waiting for a breakthrough concept to arrive one day, fully formed and ready to launch. But capitalism is not like that. Most new businesses do something pretty similar to many others – they provide familiar services or products, fulfilling a definite demand – with perhaps an incremental improvement.

You do not need an earth-shattering invention to achieve success.

Those triumphs are rare, and usually happen after

immense heartache. What you want is a solid proposition that generates sales and cash quickly, using the skills you already possess, with economics you understand, and serving a known market.

A fourth excuse is risk aversion. Too many people fear failure more than they want to win. Of course, your start-up might prove a vain attempt at the prize, so you may lose money, time and pride. But you know what? No one really notices or cares.

There is never a perfect time to begin the journey. But if you have ambition and are willing to apply the effort, stop making excuses – get out there and start battling.

Start-ups with a dash of going concern

Which is the best bet – starting a business or buying one?

That is the first great question confronting the budding entrepreneur. It's a pity so few actually ask it of themselves.

The world is in love with the romance of start-ups. The nineties dotcom boom resulted in obsessive coverage of start-ups, particularly technology start-ups, such that these days many younger entrepreneurs see no other way into business than via a newly invented gadget or service.

But all other things being equal, I believe it can

'Our greatest glory lies not in never falling, but in rising every time we fall'

Confucius

sometimes be better to buy a business than start one. I'm not necessarily talking about a large, highly profitable company – it might just be a little key money to take over an already fitted restaurant lease.

Now that advice might not be what many readers expect to hear – or want to hear – but it comes from someone who has both started businesses and bought them. Buying a business is sometimes easier in the long run.

If you buy a going concern, you will usually inherit existing customers, staff, contracts, premises, suppliers, products, brands and goodwill. All these vital elements can take years to assemble from scratch – and you may stumble on the way, possibly fatally.

The certainty and swiftness that come from taking over a project that already has momentum are worth a great deal.

In 1980 Bill Gates wanted an operating system for IBM personal computers in a hurry. So he purchased, for $75,000, exclusive rights to existing software, re-branded it as a Microsoft product and resold it to IBM. It became MS-DOS, the forerunner of Windows, and the basis of one of the largest fortunes in the world.

Buyers pay a premium for established revenues, proven technology and, sometimes, an opportunity that the founders of a business don't see.

Ray Kroc sold equipment to the McDonald brothers in their single Californian hamburger restaurant. In the brothers' fabulous formula, Kroc saw something that even the brothers themselves didn't see, and he duly developed and franchised the concept elsewhere. A few years later he bought the brothers out for $2.7 million. Before long his purchase was worth billions – built on their brainchild and his execution.

Often it is necessary to buy an operation to overcome regulatory barriers to entry: perhaps planning, licences or suchlike. To develop a mine or quarry you will probably have to agree to a lease and rights to extract minerals with a landowner. When I entered the dentistry field in 1996, we had to buy a dental body corporate, which at the time was the only legal way for a non-dentist to trade as a dental practice in the UK. Over the following years, these obscure vehicles multiplied in value tenfold as more entrants bid up their prices.

You may feel you lack the capital to buy a business. My experience has been that if you find a good enough deal, the funds will flow.

You need a degree of credibility and persistence, but the world is actually awash with capital looking for a decent return. And raising backing for an up-and-running venture is usually easier than for an entirely novel project. Veteran angels know the road to achievement is paved with defeated attempts.

Finding a worthwhile company to buy takes considerable effort. You should decide on the chosen field, and do your research thoroughly. Write, email or cold call – the worst that can happen is someone slamming the phone down.

And contact every business broker you can find. Each industry has its specialists.

Of course, purchasing another's invention does not necessarily satisfy the desire to be a genuine innovator. As inventor Nikola Tesla said: 'I do not think there is any thrill that can go through the human heart like that felt by the inventor as he sees some creation of the brain unfolding to success . . . Such emotions can make a man forget food, sleep, friends, love, everything.'

There is unquestionably a sense of purpose and passion that business founders have that is formidable to behold. And without such brilliant romantics, society would not advance.

But, as they say, many pioneers die broke. Tragically a lot of progenitors of groundbreaking schemes fail to reap the rewards of their imagination.

Charles Goodyear, popularly known as the inventor of the pneumatic tyre, never received a penny from the Goodyear Tire Company. He only received the honour of having the company named after him – and that was some forty years after his death, following his failure to win protracted patent disputes. He died $200,000 in debt.

I realize that I tend to lack the originality and obsessive temperament so common in entrepreneurs who feel compelled to build start-ups. So I aim to partner with them or invest in companies that have survived the risky early years.

Perhaps I am lazy, impatient or just unsentimental. I suppose experience has made me somewhat cynical. I have witnessed, or lost money in, so many great ideas that came to nothing that I know that a majority of new enterprises are long shots – whatever the business plans say.

Of course, if you commence with a blank sheet of paper you can compose your own dream, and as Robert Browning said, 'A man's reach should exceed his grasp, or what's a heaven for?' And you can always, on the journey, buy a business to add to your start-up.

To those readers who refuse to give a moment's thought to buying a business, I would suggest a compromise: find assets where much has been done but there remains much to do. Such projects offer reasonable odds but also the sense of exhilaration and ownership you seek from a start-up.

The correct use of optimism

As a budding entrepreneur you'll be aware that most new businesses fail in their first few years, but you can't worry about that now. You must remain optimistic.

Optimism is the oxygen necessary for progress: it is so much more than just a good mood. Optimism sparks confidence, and that fuels ambition, which in turn triggers action. It leads to new inventions, new companies, new jobs, and a higher standard of living. Without this sense of hope in the future, life is a grim affair.

Optimism is an elemental lust for life, an amazing but intangible force. It cannot be easily understood by scientific investigation, but it can surely be nurtured or discouraged, and it is up to each of us, every day, to decide if we want to look forward in hope or fear.

Important initiatives always require a leap of faith. I tend to find that those who are over-analytical struggle to make real breakthroughs. They focus so much on the downsides, they forget about the potential of the sunlit uplands. With every major decision, there will always be a moment that you approach the precipice: do you take the plunge or walk away?

It is self-evident that emotion plays a major part in such matters. Most entrepreneurs I know love to believe they are solidly rational, especially when considering dramatic steps such as a new product launch.

But the truth is that when it comes to the crunch, entrepreneurs by nature allow the animal spirits to surge, and tend to seize an opportunity. After all, no deal is ever a sure-fire thing – every innovation carries with it the chance of blunder – but for those enterprising souls, the desire for gain overwhelms the fear of loss.

Unquestionably the adrenaline rush of momentous events can lead to reckless behaviour. But winners in the game of capitalism calibrate the odds before they charge, reckoning they can cope even if it all proves a mistake. I am all for proper enquiry beforehand, and sensible hedging where practical. But never demand a certainty: if you wait for that, you will be on the sidelines for ever.

I have certainly had my episodes of despondency. It's all too easy to imprison oneself in gloom. If it's not doomsayer economists, then it's environmentalists filling us with despair or a beleaguered media industry delivering only bad news.

But such depressing predictions do not allow for the relentless tide of mankind's ingenuity, and the sheer power of positive thinking. I cannot account for it, but enthusiasm, willpower and force of personality can achieve remarkable feats.

Plenty have suffered setbacks on the road to entrepreneurial success, but short of death or prison, such reverses can always be overcome in time. Millions have been made redundant, lost their business or money or even their home – but these are not ultimate tragedies. The ultimate tragedy is to give up.

Psychology has an element of self-fulfilment about it. Plan for failure and you will surely not be disappointed. But concentrate on your strengths and apply yourself, and something heroic may emerge. Just remember that every year spring returns, that all our troubles turn into valuable experience over time, and that the world is more forgiving than you might imagine.

I like the company of entrepreneurs precisely because it is in their nature to be optimists. It's a necessary precondition of spending your life chasing dreams. If you don't know any entrepreneurs, immerse yourself in entrepreneur biographies. You'll find plenty of tribulations followed by happy endings. One can hardly avoid the rags-to-riches stories pushed by celebrity entrepreneurs, but I find the less well-known examples of optimism and true grit to be more authentic and encouraging.

Take Robert Chesebrough. He was a British-born chemist who patented petroleum jelly, which he discovered in the late 1850s, at the age of twenty-two in Titusville, Pennsylvania. It took him *ten more years* to perfect the compound, and even then nobody wanted to buy it. So he became a travelling salesman, giving away free samples of his product, which he named Vaseline. He even used to inflict burns on himself to demonstrate the soothing powers of his miracle gel.

Eventually the public took to his invention, and he became a wealthy industrialist on a major scale, with operations in dozens of countries. His persistence, self-belief and positive thinking paid off, and he lived to the age of ninety-six to enjoy the fruits of his success.

Before you begin your journey, or if you should find yourself contemplating failure, it's important to note that there are many stories like Chesebrough's. Of course, business is replete with failures too, but knowing that won't help. To dwell upon failure is to risk bringing failure upon oneself.

The true value of ideas

Most of us mistakenly believe that good business ideas occur only to the talented few, or are the product of chance. Perhaps that's because entrepreneurs love to recount the moment they were visited by the blinding flash of inspiration. It all makes for good copy. But it also adds to the notion that 'the idea' is the thing, and that every entrepreneur must have a good idea to succeed.

Budding entrepreneurs often ask me to recommend a good business idea. I do have a view – I note that people will always need to eat, for example; and that whatever works in America often works over here

'Life affords no higher pleasure than that of surmounting difficulties, passing from one step of success to another, forming new wishes and seeing them gratified'

Samuel Johnson

– but generally my advice is that you might as well pick something you already know and love. Working for yourself is a hard slog regardless of idea or sector, and you will need every bit of your knowledge and enthusiasm. That's why I'm reluctant to invest in individuals who cast themselves as 'generalist managers': give me industry veterans any day.

If you're still struggling to generate ideas, I can recommend a wonderful little book called *A Technique for Producing Ideas* (McGraw-Hill, 2003). It can be read in an hour. An advertising copywriter called James Webb Young wrote it in the 1940s.

Its formula is simple and applicable to many sorts of problem. The central premise is that any new idea is in fact only a fresh combination of old elements, and the ability to see new relationships between known facts. To produce ideas, Mr Young suggested a series of five steps.

First, you gather basic information – both general and specific – about the product or conundrum. Young was aware that sounds simplistic, but he had an eye on the procrastinators of this world: '[Fact -gathering] is such a terrible chore that we are constantly trying to dodge it . . . most of us stop too soon in the process of getting it.' He likened the process of gathering information to the advice once given to the writer De Maupassant: 'Go out into the streets of Paris and pick a cab driver. He will look to you very much like every other cab driver. But study him until you can describe him so that he is seen in your description to be an individual, different from every other cab driver in the world.'

Next you need to ponder the facts so collected,

for which Young advised 'listening to the meaning' rather than looking for it. This will eventually result in mental exhaustion, at which point the thinker has arrived at the third stage: rest! *Forget the matter temporarily*; and distract yourself with something else entirely – much as Sherlock Holmes would deliberately halt work on a difficult case and attend a concert, to the annoyance of the more logical Watson. As Young puts it, you've done the mastication, now you must stimulate the digestion.

Then follows the Eureka! moment, when an unexpected answer presents itself to you. This should come out of the blue, delivered after the mind has mulled over the issue. And the final stage is where you examine and test the idea, and improve it.

And if Young's approach doesn't work, leave behind the notion of the big idea and just do what most successful entrepreneurs do: copy and improve.

Julian Metcalfe and Sinclair Beecham did not invent the sandwich, but they did invent the premium sandwich retailer Pret A Manger. One might think that there is nothing new to bring to the world of sandwiches, but Metcalfe and Beecham thought otherwise and are now reportedly £50 million richer for it.

Seemingly small factors can differentiate a brand from the crowd and provide a competitive advantage.

When I launched the pizza restaurant chain Strada, I offered free bottles of filtered water on the table. It was a modest gesture, and hardly a major leap forward in the dining experience, but no one else was doing it at the time and diners remembered it.

Imitate first, and then devote yourself to constant

incremental improvement. You'll find your daily lot might be easier than that of the inventor, who must struggle with prototypes, patent law and an ever-cautious public.

Saying it v. doing it

Of course, theoretical concepts are all very well, but what every successful business needs is competent execution.

Management consultants have introduced devices like brainstorming and mind mapping to help foster creativity among staff within a business. They can be effective, but the most remarkable advance in recent times has been feedback from the web via digital communities and social networks.

Companies are increasingly using their customers to design their products and improve their offerings. This trend is subject to the usual raft of business jargon and dubious gurus, but it all boils down to the same advice: use the web to listen to your customers, and don't just listen – act.

I've known a customer to sit in one of my Giraffe restaurants and use Twitter to vent their dissatisfaction about the service they'd received – while they're still in the restaurant – and for my staff to detect, acknowledge and handle that complaint in person *before the customer had paid and left.*

The digital age is a boon for new products and services, for those who would truly listen to customers.

But harvesting ideas is not the hard part. Ultimately you cannot patent an idea and protect it from replication by a rival. You have to *implement* the idea – only then does it become an invention.

For innovations to work, they have to be carried out in a determined manner. That is easier for an owner-leader than for an organization with diffuse power. Large corporations are not well suited to creative breakthroughs, despite all their spending on research and development. Committees tend to resist threats to the status quo, because the new often disrupts the old.

A small, emerging company has the great advantage of flexibility. It will be willing to try new ways of doing things: new products, new services, and new ways to save costs. That is where ideas come in: they are the raw material of change – and the only fuel needed to generate them is imagination.

What's in a name?

If you want to give a person, company or product a decent start in life, take some trouble to christen them properly.

Names are always important. The power of words – how they sound, how they look, what connotations they bring – should never be underestimated.

So, how to pick a good name for your business?

Firstly, resolve to employ your imagination. Do *not* choose the lazy alternative by going straight for the predictable option every time, nor a name that comes quickly and 'feels right': Google will soon reveal that you're not the first to think of it.

If there is heritage in your product then use it, but only where it is appropriate. I cannot understand why some American men give children their own Christian name with the appendage 'Jr.'. How will the sons ever escape their shadows?

Similarly, while chairman of Channel 4 I noted the desperate lack of creativity at ITV in calling their digital channels ITV2, ITV3 and ITV4. What differentiates one from the others? What does each channel mean to the viewer or advertiser? I haven't yet met anyone at ITV who can tell me.

Whenever you can, make sure a name has some underlying meaning. Don't copy the example of Diageo, one of the world's biggest drinks manufacturers. 'Diageo' means nothing. It's not even easy to spell, or to Google. The bigwigs at Diageo – the company formerly known as Guinness – thought their new name had more international appeal than the legendary Irish stout, but what's wrong with being associated with one of the most famous beers in the world? For everything that's bad about high-concept names, look no further than Diageo's own toe-curling explanation: 'The word Diageo comes from the Latin for day (*dia*) and the Greek for world (*geo*). We take this to mean every day, everywhere, people celebrate with our brands.' I wonder if Diageo's management realize that having to listen to that sort of rot could well make its staff want to quit and start their own business.

Some years ago I helped assemble a company called Bath Press PLC from an existing company founded by Isaac Pitman (of shorthand fame) in the nineteenth century. Once the company expanded, it grandly re-named itself Liberfabrica – apparently the Latin for book printing. No one could spell it or knew what it meant. Sadly it was a name too clever by half, and the City never really took to it, so in due course the business was sold to the French.

Holding companies – firms that exist solely to own other firms, such as Warren Buffett's Berkshire Hathaway – are forever struggling with their identities. While I was a governor of The London Institute ('What the hell is *that*?' you might ask) we renamed the organization University of the Arts London. Suddenly the world began to realize we were the body comprising the best of London's art colleges – Central St Martins, Camberwell, London College of Communication, London College of Fashion, Wimbledon and Chelsea. It became clear what we did and where we were. I am convinced the rebranding has strengthened the institution and enhanced its status.

Avoid being too precious, obscure or stuffy about names. The French wine industry has lost export market share to New World rivals partly because the former has clung on to its complex system for designating wine, while the newcomers are more adventurous in their product names. But some growers are beginning to learn: one of the fastest-growing French whites in the US is called Fat Bastard Chardonnay. It shows that a human, quirky name will beat an academic or artificial one every time.

Names should be simple to say and understand where possible. Strada, the pizzeria chain I founded, is a very Italian word and easy to spell and pronounce.

Despite the plethora of products and services, there are still good, resonant names to be found if you make the effort, as did the firms behind BlackBerry, Viagra and YouTube. While the Internet has intensified the competition for good names, it has also amplified their value: a Google-friendly name is a real asset.

Of course, managers are forever discarding well-established brand names – and all their attached good-will – for petty reasons of ego or just change for its own sake. Advertising and design agencies are skilled at persuading clients to spend huge sums on new re-brand and launch campaigns. You hear excuses about 'coherence of corporate identity' or 'economies of scale' but this is mostly cant.

When I was a stockbroker in the 1980s I saw al-most all the finest, long-established broking houses gobbled up by banks and their revered names unnec-essarily thrown away – like my old firm Grieveson Grant. No wonder few of the buyers achieved much value for their acquisitions. The ultimate goal of any name is to be noticed and remembered, lest they meet the fate William Cowper ascribed to certain names in the *Biographia Britannica*:

'Oh, fond attempt to give a deathless lot
To names ignoble, born to be forgot!'

Is this a good time to start a business?

'If you have the urge to do your own thing, then prevailing interest rates, stock market highs and lows, unemployment figures and housing statistics will make not a jot of difference as to whether your tiny insignificant company will succeed or not'
Jon Hunt, founder of the Foxtons estate-agency chain, started for £30,000 in a recession-bound 1981; sold for £390 million in 2007

If you're in a position to pick and choose when to become an entrepreneur, consider yourself unlucky. You risk becoming one of those unfortunates who find a reason to put it off for ever.

I concede that starting – or buying – a business during a boom probably feels less scary than in a recession, when many would-be entrepreneurs prefer to hunker down in their day jobs. If you've the luxury of wondering whether now is the right time to be an entrepreneur, you're possibly at a disadvantage to single parents, school-leavers and the newly fired, all of whom must figure out some way to pay the bills whatever the weather.

Absent a salary, some must start their own business out of sheer necessity – but at least they get going. I've mentioned that ambition is crucial to the entrepreneur, and nothing saps ambition quite like a steady income.

But there are lessons to be had from the booms and busts of previous eras.

In particular, you should consider your options before jumping onto bandwagon businesses. To that end I can recommend *Devil Take the Hindmost* by Edward Chancellor (Macmillan, 2000), for its fine introduction to the subject of wild booms and busts through the ages. The author is an ex-Lazard merchant banker who understands his material. His book covers a grand sweep from the Dutch tulip-mania of the 1630s to the Japanese bubble economy of the 1980s. It shows that when it comes to making investments, we are doomed to endlessly repeat our mistakes.

Every era brings forth innovations, which offer great reward and attract risk capital. The substantial initial profits encourage a rush of capital and company valuations get out of control. Things then inevitably come down to earth, with drastic suffering the result. Our age invents new phrases, but human greed and crowd psychology are a constant.

In Chancellor's book, phrases from hundreds of years ago might have been uttered today. In 1826, following the collapse of many South American projects floated on the London market, a magazine called them 'a great shoal of monstrous abortions – begotten by fraud upon credulity!' One wonders how many US sub-prime mortgage loans fell into this category.

The book debates whether the speculative instinct is conducive to human progress. There is no doubt that on occasion rampant speculation can divert resources and effort from productive uses and lead to waste, loss and misery. In 1845 the euphoria in Britain surrounding the building of railways was such that it placed unbearable demands on the country's economy.

Over 1,200 projects were proposed, with liabilities exceeding the national income. It led to a major crisis in 1847, with competing lines, uneconomic routes and squandered capital.

More recently, the wild property and share speculation in Japan in the 1980s helped create the horrific pile of perhaps $1.5 trillion of bad loans in their banking system. Cheap money stimulated pointless over-investment, which has added to the woes. This reckless squandering has seen Japan's economy steadily slither into virtual slump, record levels of unemployment, decimated share and property markets and a painful credit crunch.

Chancellor's book quotes the extraordinary story of Mrs Onoue, a lowly Osaka restaurateur who in the midst of the bubble was allowed to borrow a total of $23 billion to buy shares. Reportedly her portfolio was controlled by a ceramic toad, which was said to receive trading tips from the gods. It was quite a draw at her restaurant.

One is constantly reminded that during periods of rapidly rising prosperity, people start behaving strangely and believing odd things. My point is that the desire to gamble and take risk is innate, and will always be with us. After all, without gamblers, who would set up in business and throw up security for gain? Society needs chancers if it is to keep moving – and it must throw money at them from time to time.

Such tendencies will lead to regular bouts of excess and then wreckage, but, like so much else at the beginning of one's entrepreneurial journey, you can't worry about that now. You must begin regardless.

Now, to understand the business cycle is to better understand how the parts of capitalism fit together, so I'll examine business cycles in greater detail later on. Let's just say today is a better time to start a business than tomorrow, no matter how today looks.

John Maynard Keynes put it well: 'The thought of ultimate loss which overtakes pioneers, as experience undoubtedly tells us and them, is put aside as a healthy man puts aside the expectation of death.'

Others are insulated by more prosaic means: when Jon Hunt started Foxtons he had recently left army service, and was so green about business affairs that he 'didn't even know' that there was a recession on! I suspect he knew a little more about the cycle when he came to sell Foxtons, at the very peak of the global property boom in 2007.

To the recent graduate

I graduated in 1983, straight into the aftermath of an economic recession. From 1979 to 1984, UK unemployment *doubled*. At the time the country was undergoing painful but necessary change, as the Thatcher government implemented a spell of tough spending cuts in order to reboot the UK economy. Company earnings fell.

Anyone graduating at that time might have felt that they were particularly unlucky. Since recessions will always be with us, it's possible that the reader is graduating into a recession right now.

'Youth has the resilience to absorb disaster and weave it into the pattern of its life, no matter how anguishing the thorn that penetrates its flesh'

Sholem Asch, Jewish novelist

If so, don't let it bother you.

It's true that a graduate finishing university during a downturn will likely join large numbers of other graduates in a spell of unemployment, unable to climb onto the conventional career ladder. They will be competing with thousands of older, more experienced candidates who have been made redundant.

They are likely to leave college with high debts, high self-esteem and high expectations – which are equally likely to be dashed. They will be full of hopes about an interesting and well-rewarded job, perhaps in a green and sustainable workplace – all of which will be irrelevant when they can't get work, or certainly not one of the high-flying jobs they all dreamed about.

Perhaps the first step for many will be to defer the agony and travel the world for a year or so, living on little and earning while they can. I never embarked on such a venture, and sometimes I do regret not taking more time off when young and living abroad. But I was too keen to get started and find my place in the world. Patience has never been a great virtue of mine.

The alternative to a gap year off wandering, assuming there are no suitable vacancies, is to become self-employed. In some ways the very best age to work for yourself is when you are young and single, with no dependants, or obligations like mortgages. Security should not matter: what is important is gaining experience and credibility.

The obvious sphere to start a business is your field of study, or your particular passion. Only you know what they are. I would counsel that you avoid the obvious markets, products and services. Aim for the obscure, the boring, the poorly researched, the niche, the undesirable, or the ugly opportunities. These are places the crowds miss. All this may conflict with your passion – but then these are hard times.

What matters most is that you can turn a profit and keep going. The other overriding priority for recent graduates and school-leavers is to choose a project that requires almost no capital. I would also advise you work with a partner or two: teams are more likely to survive than sole operators.

None of this will be easy, but it may be no harder to earn a living running your own show than getting the job you really want. Typically less than one in ten run their own business; but we're moving to the era of independent and inventive freelancers. The freedom and satisfaction of being your own boss is hard to beat.

Our future depends upon youthful energy coming up with brilliant ideas to gradually solve our problems and give us all hope. I spent much of my twenties frustrated that my life as an entrepreneur wasn't taking off as I had anticipated. But I suppose I was serving a sort of apprenticeship, gathering knowledge, contacts and resources to use later on.

So I would say to those who face bleak job prospects: take the plunge, and if your schemes come to nothing, then at least you tried. The most fascinating people I've ever met are those who have seen life as an adventure, a great experiment, and managed to retain their optimism along the way.

Part 2
PEOPLE

Age and the founder

Just as there's never a perfect time to start a business – other than right now – no founder is ever at the perfect age to start.

My favourite manual on the subject of age and the entrepreneur is an out-of-print autobiography called *After I Was Sixty*, by Roy – later Lord – Thomson (Hamish Hamilton, 1975). In 1953, aged sixty, he suffered two blows. First, his wife of many decades died; then his business partner of twenty years left to run another business. So he left his modest radio company in Canada for Edinburgh and, almost on a whim, bought the struggling *Scotsman* newspaper.

A year later he founded STV, the first commercial broadcaster north of the border. It was an astounding success, making a return of at least 1,500 per cent for its original subscribers. It was he who muttered the immortal phrase describing a television franchise as a 'licence to print money' (no longer the valid statement it once was). He went on to become a pioneer backer of North Sea oil, and later launched Thomson Holidays, Britain's first package-tour operator. Subsequently he became the owner of *The Times* and the *Sunday Times*, and ultimately his organization merged with Reuters to become one of Canada's largest corporations. All this, and a peerage too, after sixty.

He's not the only late developer in business history. Harland D. Sanders had a tough childhood, going out to work at the age of twelve as a farmhand. He held a series of modest jobs until he opened a service station at the age of forty, and started serving pan-fried chicken. His 'finger-lickin' good' chicken became well known, but the property burned to the ground when he was forty-seven. He started again and built up a second success, but a new bypass took all the passing traffic away and he was forced to sell out at a knockdown price.

By now 'Colonel' Sanders was sixty-six years old and pretty broke. But he had his secret chicken recipe, and so he set out to sell the concept of Kentucky Fried Chicken as a franchise. Within four years he had signed up over 400 restaurants and it had become the world's largest take-out chicken business. Despite selling out for just $2 million in 1960, Harland Sanders remained involved with his creation and lived until he was ninety.

I am moved to comment on mature entrepreneurs by reading a study from the think-tank Reform. It revealed that one in sixteen of those aged forty-six to sixty-five hopes to embark on a new business venture rather than just retire. This would be seven times the number of start-ups from their parents' generation – and could amount to a million new businesses. Their experience and wisdom will be their secret weapon.

Ageing baby-boomers realize that collapsing pension provision and rising longevity means many will have to work until they are well past sixty. But that needn't be so bad. I am inspired by the example of my dad, Paul Johnson, who published two books aged eighty on top of the fifty he had already written. Interesting work brings a feeling of purpose at any age.

Not every venture started by a 'silver entrepreneur'

need be a for-profit undertaking. It might be a charity, a social enterprise, a civic endeavour, a new neighbourhood organization or a recreational club. We do not, after all, face a shortage of opportunities – across industry, politics or in communities. There are endless activities that could be done more efficiently, or problems to be solved. And while capital might be in short supply, human ingenuity and energy are an infinite resource.

When ageism in the workplace is clearly rife, the veteran generation can take its revenge by going freelance and doing well in the self-employed world. Or they can volunteer, or mentor younger people. It is a tremendous way to keep in touch with other generations, and to contribute knowledge. I occasionally teach a case study at London Business School, or give talks to groups of students. I find it hugely invigorating to interact with ambitious twenty-somethings, keen to learn and with a different perspective on work and life.

America has impressive initiatives such as encore. org, a campaign to encourage citizens to have a second career in later life. They award a Purpose Prize to those aged over sixty who are taking on society's biggest challenges. It is based on the recognition that, for most, a dream of golden years of endless leisure is neither fulfilling nor practical. Moreover, millions of retirees doing nothing is a vast waste of human talent. Again, my mum reinvented herself as a counsellor after she was sixty, giving her a genuine sense of renewal.

'Young men are fitter to invent than to judge; fitter for execution than counsel; and fitter for new projects than settled business'

Francis Bacon

Time, energy and ideas

But to everything there is a season. As I enter middle age I know that I have fewer fresh ideas than in the past, even if I also know that new ideas are only part of the equation.

The most fertile period for innovation is when people are in their twenties: from Nobel Prize winners, to entrepreneurs, to composers, to writers, real breakthroughs and greatest works tend to be the province of the young.

This is one more reason big companies struggle to innovate. They have hierarchies of executives who benefit from the status quo. Those who control the levers of power are mostly older, and often feel threatened by youthful up-and-comers. This ossification allows upstarts from outside to challenge and win against entrenched interests, despite all the latter's advantages. Look at how Google has usurped 'legacy' media companies, despite their wealth, strong franchises, and huge market shares.

New companies and different technologies upset the old order, so of course incumbents resist them.

We should all follow Dr Johnson's advice: make friends with those younger than ourselves – because they will still be alive when most of our contemporaries are dead – and they will inspire us to remain alive to new possibilities.

I fear after a certain age we shy away from risk, since we feel we have more downside than before. After all, at present the combined net worth of all Britons under thirty-five is zero: as the saying goes: when you got nothin', you got nothin' to lose. No wonder the Y generation put their innermost secrets on Facebook, get tattoos, and refuse to conform.

According to the Global Entrepreneurship Monitor, today's youngsters are more likely to set up their own business than previous cohorts. They probably know that job security and final salary pensions are all history. But by forty we are burdened by mortgages, the responsibilities of parenthood, and generally becoming respectable members of society. Too many assets perhaps – but do we still have enough hope?

Too many of us become progressively more cynical with age, growing sceptical, pessimistic and prone to saying 'No'. Perhaps some have experienced too many broken dreams, seen too many things go wrong.

Sadly these attitudes do not foster experimentation and progress. Throughout history, the ingenuity of man has overcome fearsome obstacles. Civilization has triumphed and progressed. The young have to believe fervently in the future – ought to believe in it – whereas perhaps some older folk don't *really* care because they will be dead by then. They might do well to recall Khalil Gibran: 'Desire is half of life; indifference is half of death.'

As we age, we accumulate experience, which is valuable. But we also accumulate bias – which means we sometimes dismiss original thoughts too easily. We think we know all the answers and have tried everything already.

The audacity and energy of youth is a necessary antidote to the caution of veterans. As we advance

'From the earliest time the old have rubbed it into the young that they are wiser, and before the young had discovered what nonsense this was they too were old, and it profited them to carry on the imposture'

Somerset Maugham

in years, we must resist the temptation to hoard our riches, just as Western nations should make intelligent bets on young blood, better to avoid the fate of Japan, where too many conservative, elderly men command everything, resisting change. By the time newcomers get to the top they are worn out and inculcated with the *ancien régime*'s defensive beliefs.

Yet many of the wisest and funniest people in business I've met have been over sixty. They possess far more patience than I do and have seen so much before.

The best among the elderly do not cling to power and assets. They involve the younger generations and work with them. They enjoy their company and make an effort to understand their enthusiasms. After all, age is really a state of mind.

I have been privileged to serve on several company boards with non-executives in their sixties and seventies, and in most cases they have been huge contributors. They tend to have time and take trouble. They have less impetuous ambition and a more balanced view. Frequently they have superb contacts built up over a lifetime of networking. And the best ones welcome as partners young capitalists in their twenties and thirties with grand visions but much to learn.

The combination of skills and outlooks is a powerful force that can help us better adapt and compete economically. After all, the 'grey' market is a huge new area that will continue expanding as people live longer and retire rich.

Only by sharing resources with those younger than us will we avoid inter-generational strife. The over-fifties may control three-quarters of the entire nation's assets, but they need the talent and insight of the younger generation to make that capital really productive. The solutions to every thorny problem – from global issues such as climate change to the personal question of maintaining vitality – can be found if the old and the young work together to foment money, creativity, wisdom and boldness. It just needs the right attitude on both sides.

Poor children of the rich and successful

Being the child of a wealthy entrepreneur must be something of a mixed blessing. Growing up in a hothouse atmosphere, full of privilege and expectation, cannot be a relaxing experience.

I spend most of my time working with entrepreneurs, and I really believe that they are not the same as other people. They have an ambition, a competitive urge and a lust to take risks that is way beyond the norm.

I met Rupert Murdoch, Jimmy Goldsmith and Richard Branson on separate occasions in my late teens and wondered what they were like as businessmen and, even more, as fathers. Exciting, no doubt – but how much were they actually there for their children? And what did they expect from them?

The pressure on the offspring of very rich, self-made

people to achieve must be intense. Inevitably, the second generation tend to find their parents a tough act to follow. Most tycoons like the idea of their children running their empires when they are dead; I suppose part of it is a subconscious desire for immortality.

Often such hopes are doomed. Perhaps an heir or heiress feels that their father or mother paid too high a price for success; perhaps they want to strike out on their own, to show independence; or perhaps the business was always destined to fade, and the inheritor can sense that they will be unable to match their parent's glories. In any case, as Aldous Huxley reminds us, 'Sons have always a rebellious wish to be disillusioned by that which charmed their fathers.'

For whatever reason, family companies in the twenty-first century rarely make a smooth transition from their founder's grasp. More often than not they are sold, for fear that no one can match the original boss. Of course, that too can induce bitterness: I know of two entrepreneurs who feel that they were swindled out of their birthright by cowardly relatives and slippery lawyers, who sold the family firm.

Many captains of industry are liable to lose their assets at some point in a venture that goes wrong. Their sons and daughters have no choice but to adjust to the swing in fortune. Falling property prices and high debts forced a property-developer friend of mine to go from a town house in central London's Belgravia and Home Counties estate to rented accommodation in a gritty part of South London – with wife and son in tow. Without doubt he will be back before long.

Some children copy their parents' irrepressible

optimism and confidence, and embrace a life chasing their dreams. Others do the opposite and pursue an existence of quiet caution, reacting to the restless roller coaster of their early years. But at least having to adapt to both plenty and scarcity makes for a more versatile upbringing than one of remorseless overindulgence.

Every parent wants something better for their children than they had. Thus, many entrepreneurs, born with a hunger for recognition and material advancement, spoil their daughters and sons.

This tendency in itself must blunt any urge in their children to build a fantastically profitable business. Who needs to struggle if they have been given everything? I know one billionaire family who have managed to instil a sense of proportion, industry and obligation into the younger members: there are no private jets, chauffeurs or suchlike. Instead each generation acts as true custodian of the family's business, and most dividend income appears to go to philanthropic causes rather than on personal spending.

Such willpower and self-denial is rare – sad cases like the Rockefellers and Hiltons are more common.

Driven characters tend to work long hours and, as a consequence, are at home with their families less. Such absence can mean strained relationships and endless guilt. In previous eras, most fathers saw much less of their children; but now society demands they play a much bigger role in parenting, and so there are conflicts. Sacrifices generally have to be made for unusual success – whichever career path one follows.

For those inventors and corporate pioneers whose life is their business, it is all too clear where their ultimate priorities lie. Too bad for them: almost every entrepreneur I have known regrets not spending enough time with their children when they were growing up.

Joys and perils of a partnership

Entrepreneurship can be a lonely affair, and that's one reason that I have worked with partners my entire business career. Being your own boss is eternally appealing; being your own colleague less so.

For me, it has always been preferable to share the journey than to direct matters as a sole trader. Perhaps I have made less money than I might have but I believe the experience has been more fun, and I've got involved in far more projects than I could have working alone. Besides, very few of us have the genius of a Henry Ford or Sam Walton: for most of us, a partnership will improve the odds of success.

A partner helps relieve the isolation of being the boss and the stress of judging risks. While firms cannot function as democracies, pure dictatorships are vulnerable to all the whims and failings of an individual personality, such as overreach, emotional fragility, intellectual limitations and favouritism.

The easiest partnership is a 50/50 deal, each contributing the same capital and effort, and starting at the same point in the life of an enterprise. But such arrangements may well not be feasible or fair. Often one party has more cash or time or know-how, or has already initiated the operation.

Either way it means the partnership will not be equal, but that should not undermine its success as long as there is mutual respect, complementary skills and aligned objectives.

Most partnerships have a life span. My old colleague at PizzaExpress, David Page, reckoned the typical set-up lasts ten years; I think it varies according to the circumstances. The trigger for dissolution is usually the sale of the joint undertaking. Frequently, one side has the urge to continue the chase, while the other wants to sit back and enjoy their wealth.

Sometimes it is death, divorce or simply diverging priorities that lead to a break-up. As with marriage, ideally such partings are not rancorous; but envy and festering resentments mean bitterness and litigation can flare up when things finish.

There are many talent pairings. I like the combination of an accountant and a salesperson. Other great teams can comprise smooth negotiator and hard nut (a Mr Nice and a Mr Nasty), or a brilliant creative brain matched with a first-class commercial mind.

So often the prime mover is an inventor of some sort, while the partner brings street smarts or finance, or simply energy and confidence.

Curiously, companies hiring high-level staff will undertake extensive referencing and even psychometric testing to ensure the candidate's suitability for a post, but few entrepreneurs will carry out much rigorous analysis when going into partnership with someone.

All too often we fall into business with someone because we enjoy their company or because we are friends, when the best qualifications are that a person is competent and reliable in business matters.

Partnerships are most vital when times are tough. There is no substitute for being able to discuss confidential affairs in detail with a colleague of equal rank and understanding. Advisors, subordinates, spouses and friends are simply not as likely to be as engaged – or as honest.

For many entrepreneurs, forging a partnership defeats the purpose of working for oneself. It means you cannot control your own destiny to the same degree and take the same level of pride, credit and creative satisfaction. But most of us accept we have shortcomings, and realize that an equity partner will try harder and bring more to the relationship than any employee.

But like any marriage, partnerships must be handled and worked at. They go wrong with alarming frequency. It's always a terrible thing to witness, and it can happen to the best.

In an interview John Lennon gave in 1970, soon after the break-up of the Beatles, he described why things went wrong for surely one of the most wonderful partnerships ever. He was scathing about the egos of his fellow band members and their envy towards him and hatred of Yoko Ono. Unparalleled success didn't prevent even the Fab Four from a bitter fall-out, and separately Paul, John, George and Ringo never saw the heights they enjoyed as a group. It reminded me of how winning teams in business usually end up going their separate ways, often in rancour.

Three things in particular can precipitate corporate divorce. Firstly, achievement changes people. Once someone attains status and wealth, their attitude towards sharing the spoils and the glory alters. It slowly dawns on them that actually all the clever moves and breakthroughs were *their* idea, and in fact they are the only one who really does any work. So of course they believe they deserve more of the applause. Thus resentments set in and eventually the bust-up occurs.

Very often memories of the early days get confused. People claim credit for the work or ideas of others – forgetting how much they needed support in the beginning. I have frequently seen deals where the initial carve-up of the spoils leads to trouble later: but at the time that was the arrangement. Those terms were right for the moment. Regret is a dangerous tendency.

The second factor is that as people age their personal situation evolves. They usually get married, have a family and develop a new set of priorities in life. Spouses and children become far more important to a founder than their business and the partnership that created it. They make some money, the hunger and ambition abate, and perhaps they decide to give up all the striving for a more settled life.

Illness can also intervene. At both Microsoft and Apple, a single founder of each remains involved and famous: Bill Gates and Steve Jobs. But in each case there was a co-founder who dropped out through ill-health (Paul Allen and Steve Wozniak respectively). The fact is that running large organizations takes real stamina and many find the intensity and responsibilities too onerous.

Failure tends to bring out the knives. Everyone starts blaming someone else for the problems. It amazes me how often chief executives get away with the argument that they were not money men, and that the finance director was the only person who understood what went wrong and why the cash ran out. With all the recriminations of a bust-up, litigation usually follows. As ever, the lawyers are the big winners.

But enough about break-ups: what about the getting together part? How on earth do partners meet? Often it seems they come together almost randomly. I first met one of my business partners, Gary Ashworth, in the early 1990s when I tried and failed to buy his recruitment business; I met my partner Paul May when I invested in the retail company he ran.

William Hewlett met David Packard when they both played for the Stanford football team. Charles Rolls, the aristocratic motor trader, met the engineer Henry Royce through a mutual friend called Henry Edmunds at the Midland Hotel, Manchester, in 1904.

Given that random chance seems to be a key factor in establishing great partnerships, perhaps the best advice I can give to those who would pair up is to get out from behind the desk and constantly place yourself in serendipity's way. In short, network.

Networking

There is much to be said for gatherings where business owners can share their war stories or hear new ideas. Once upon a time the Chamber of Commerce or the Rotary Club filled this role. Before them, perhaps even the gentlemen's clubs of St James's or the country clubs of Florida and the Hamptons. But these are no longer enough.

Newer generations of business leaders can find these organizations a little stuffy and old fashioned. In response I founded the Mandrake Club, a free monthly get-together in London for those running companies. The format was deliberately simple and informal. It was an occasion to network: to find deals, investors, partners, new recruits, clients, suppliers and so forth. I launched it because I felt there was nowhere for entrepreneurs to exchange knowledge and gain inspiration from like-minded individuals. The club continues to this day.

In the twenty-first century, these forums have moved online. Nowadays many executives connect via sites such as Linkedin.com, which claims hundreds of millions of users across 200 countries.

Personally I think these sites lack something by being purely online: I believe online networking cannot replace the connection you make when actually meeting someone face to face. Of course an initial contact via the net can lead to contact in person; but at heart these are tools and nothing more. There are also genuine privacy worries with these digital networks – they are no substitute for personal references from a real friend – to say nothing of the real motivation of some members. Many are only there to spam others.

For me the ideal entrepreneurs' network is small and local, with a changing line-up to keep it fresh. It should be non-profit and unfussy, with an emphasis on the partners interacting to their mutual advantage, and perhaps an ancillary role of charitable giving. Ideally it covers all sectors and ages, with veterans giving tips to up-and-comers. There should be start-ups, family firms and established companies. Building a business is never easy, and the best support always comes from those who have been there before. Just beware Adam Smith's famous dictum: 'People of the same trade seldom meet together, even for merriment and diversion, but the conversation ends in a conspiracy against the public, or in some contrivance to raise prices.' These days that's a criminal offence.

Cliques and clubs – the ties that bind

It seems every profession has a small circle of characters that basically command things. In most industries, you can fit them round a table. After all, in mature economies most markets are dominated by a handful of operators – if you assemble the owners, founders and heads of those companies, it would often be fewer than twenty people.

There is mutual respect and occasional cooperation between these bosses – but is there plotting against the consumer? Adam Smith thought so, but I disagree. It's more likely that the members of such groups spend their time conspiring against each other.

At the sharp end, business leaders compete ferociously for power, fame, money, market share, staff, property and awards. And, as Smith said, once more: 'Rivalship and emulation render excellency and frequently occasion the very greatest exertions.' Their personal and corporate ambition militates against monopolies by sowing discord among the clique.

It would be interesting to chart how long the various figures tend to remain in charge. I guess the majority of up-and-comers get asked to sup at the head table around the age of forty. If they do well or exhaust themselves, they may well feel like easing off at fifty-five. But for fifteen years or more they should be calling the shots – unless they blow it. And since there are only so many seats around the table, barring an industry upset, the cast changes are normally pretty slow, prompted by a retirement or the occasional upstart come to stake their claim with the Big Boys (or Girls).

In highly entrepreneurial sectors such as the restaurant trade, most executives are there because they have created or transformed a business. In the years since I was part of a group that took control of Pizza-Express, members of that team have been involved in a raft of firms in Britain, including Strada, Gourmet Burger Kitchen, Patisserie Valerie, Giraffe, Wagamama,

Belgo, Tootsies and others. A family tree would show interrelationships between all these organizations.

At first glance, entrepreneurs by their nature are not exactly clubbable types. There is a popular view of them as independent-minded loners who set out to build a world of their own, apart from the crowd. Yet they are mostly extroverts who need regularly to socialize and swap business cards.

The budding entrepreneur should give vent to the need to socialize, and capitalize upon it in others. Again, my advice is to leave your desk and start networking. You're unlikely to stumble across a Masonic-like association whose members secretly gather to cheat their customers, but if you know where to look, you will find significant concentrations of power, contacts and know-how that you can use to your benefit.

Mentoring

It's lonely being the boss of a company, be it in good times or in crisis. There is nowhere to run. It can get surprisingly desolate up there on the bridge, trying to captain the ship through the storm. You have to make the difficult decisions. And you get the blame if it all goes wrong.

In PLCs there are boards of directors, and probably a chairman to offer wise counsel to the chief executive. But in a private business there is rarely someone of substance to advise the entrepreneur running things. Of course they chose to be the leader, to take command and to call the shots. Nevertheless, from time to time even the broadest shoulders need an encouraging word, an intelligent listener, and a trusted ally. Because as Chekhov wrote, 'People who lead a lonely existence always have something on their minds they are eager to talk about.'

The modern management industry has coined words like mentoring and coaching to describe what is really an ancient art. This recent terminology may be an excuse for armies of consultants to charge executives hefty fees for a little bit of nurturing that they could probably obtain elsewhere for nothing.

From time immemorial, those in charge have sought a confidant to whom they can unburden the woes of high office, and discuss hard choices. Someone honest and discreet, someone who understands, someone who offers a veteran's perspective on matters of business – and life. This is not therapy, or some sort of clinical treatment. It is an occasional boost to one's confidence and a word of caution from an experienced player who has done it all before. In my view it is closer to philosophy than management waffle.

My earliest mentor was probably Dr John Stein, my university tutor. He stood by me when I should have been thrown out for failing my first-year exams, and was enthusiastic about me pursuing a commercial career once it was obvious medicine was not my vocation. Over the decades I have been lucky enough to be able to call on various partners and friends as sounding boards and supporters, figures to whom one could turn in moments of isolation. And now and then, in turn, I have attempted to help aspiring entrepreneurs in their endeavours, always starting with my golden rule: never give a personal guarantee (more on that later).

The founder's passion

There is an elemental life force present in the founder of a business. To give birth to an important new enterprise takes a special sort of genius and courage. Inventors, creators – they are different from managers, investors and inheritors. My late relative Tom Cassidy, the legendary toymaker, was one of these rare people.

Tom trained as a toolmaker and started by making tiny skating boots in a shed at the back of his mum's house in 1945. By 1950 his brother Joe had joined him and the partners registered the brand name Casdon. Six years later their company Cassidy Brothers Limited moved to a purpose-built factory in Blackpool. It eventually became the largest manufacturer in the town. The business came to specialize in the production of miniaturized versions of household appliances for children. It went public in 1989, and remains a quoted company, although it is in essence a family business.

Tom was a larger-than-life character with a great sense of humour and extraordinary energy. The toy industry is incredibly seasonal and volatile, but Cassidy Brothers has enjoyed over fifty years of success – a rare feat in an ultra-competitive field that is dominated by foreign firms. To me Tom epitomized the chutzpah of the self-made founder: full of confidence, adaptability, personality and a sort of irresistible grandeur.

On a larger scale, I would call Henry Ford a classic founder. His vision – mass production of a cheap automobile for Everyman – was truly groundbreaking. He too started out as an engineer, eventually running Edison Illuminating's factory in Detroit. In 1899, at the age of thirty-six, he left to run his own car workshop. Initially he had partners, but with growth Ford was able to squeeze out his co-shareholders, and he became majority owner of the Ford Motor Company in 1904.

His really big winner, the Model T, was launched in October 1908, for $825. It soon became a by-word for the successful application of the mass assembly techniques instituted by Ford himself. By the end of the First World War, almost half the cars in the world were Model Ts, a quite astounding achievement.

Henry Ford exhibited all the traits of great founders: imagination, diligence, and popularity – as well as autocracy. He was single minded in pursuit of expansion. He fought a huge legal battle over a patent that purported to cover all petrol-powered vehicles. He won a resounding victory on appeal, and freed the entire automotive industry from paying millions of dollars of royalties every year to a greedy banking syndicate. Later he took up extreme political causes, and allowed his business to drift, but despite his flaws he was the greatest automotive entrepreneur of all time.

Over the decades, while Ford has remained under family control, the founder's commercial and technical genius overshadowed all his successors, to the point where the business today has on occasion struggled for its very survival. Henry's son Edsel initially took over from his father, but he failed to cope, and died aged just forty-nine. Other descendants have enjoyed varying success as leaders of Ford, a dynasty unable to escape the influence of its founder's remarkable tenacity and ambition.

No one can ever supplant a founder. The founder's passion and insight are unique, and managerial structures never have the same raw energy and conviction that the progenitor brings to his or her undertaking.

Families in particular have difficulty evolving a business after the departure of a patriarch. This might be because even if they've retired, the founder hasn't really left – or perhaps because his son (and it's usually father and son) can't stop asking himself: 'I wonder what Dad would have thought of this?' They often preserve their father's legacy – whereas in truth the founder was the sort to upset the old order and create anew.

Those who inherit tend to assume a caretaker's attitude, and lack the audacity and ruthlessness of a founder. And managers do not possess the same emotional intensity that enables a founder to overcome such huge obstacles.

Many of the most fascinating people I have ever known are business founders: difficult, demanding, even impossible – but brilliant.

The greatest founders are also outstanding motivators – they know how to enthuse their partners and workforce with a passion for the business. They do this with charisma, financial incentives, hard work, domain knowledge and by leading from the front.

Founders earn respect through an ability to listen, and to spot talent and build on the strengths of others. Founders do not seize all the limelight: they give fair credit to their team, and congratulate those who do well.

Bottom-up management

Most successful entrepreneurs face a time when they must either hire a people manager or become one. It is impossible to overstate the importance of good management, or the difficulties associated with it.

Just as you meet few truly great individuals in the journey through life, so too I have met only a modest number of outstanding managers. The reason few organizations are really well run is not that it is a complicated matter; it is that managing well takes more discipline and effort than most managers possess. Good management practice is often just common sense, but the managers have something else: deep-seated values.

I can recommend *The Puritan Gift* by Kenneth and William Hopper (I. B. Tauris, 2009). It is one of the best management books I have read in years. It is a work of history, showing how the values which underpinned America's extraordinary growth in the twentieth century, such as energy, competitiveness and a capacity for innovation, originated in the personal ethos of America's first wave of immigrants.

It also functions as a study of how the Anglo-American financial system, which is losing those values, has gone wrong. The book should be required reading for everyone who cares about the capitalist system and those in high office in the business world.

All the best companies have bottom-up management. That means those staff who actually meet customers, or run operations, tell the boss what works, rather than vice versa. It means delegating responsibility in order to empower staff.

Imperious, dictatorial leaders who are out of touch with the shop floor do not achieve sustained success. I was told of the chief executive of a large publisher who, when the fire alarm went off accidentally, would summon his chauffeur to pick him up so he could circle the building ensconced in his limousine rather than stand on the pavement and mingle with the troops. Not surprisingly, the business underperformed and he was replaced.

Another characteristic of top managers is that they manage for the long term.

Sudden strategic moves to suit quarterly targets or shorter-term bonus measures are damaging. Family stewardship often beats publicly traded or private equity as a form of ownership for this reason. Germany's Mittelstand companies, which are principally family owned, are the backbone of their economy: often world-class operations that adopt prudent financing, and invest in capital expenditure and research and development. Incentives at all levels tend to be long term.

The best managers have real domain knowledge. This means they understand their industry and are experts in their field. It allows them to command the respect of their colleagues, and means they have genuine insight into the vital economics of their profession or niche.

When I interview managers, I ask them about their customers and competitors. The high achievers will know them intimately, and can talk for hours about the strengths and weaknesses of their rivals. Generic managers, who claim they can turn their skills to any sector and deliver impressive results, are mostly a clever illusion. That is why I tend to respect actual experience in a line of work, or a specific trade qualification, over an MBA.

Companies I've most admired have usually been run by teams. While every business needs an ultimate boss, larger twenty-first-century organizations are too complex to permit an individual to call all the shots. The enduring successes have several high-quality people at the top working as a collegiate group, cooperating and sharing responsibilities across divisions and disciplines.

The most able executives find, nurture and retain talent, and they delegate and congratulate in large doses.

They never promote sycophants; instead they hire ambitious challengers who can one day replace them.

A further characteristic of outperformers is that they seek constant improvement through small but material steps – a process sometimes referred to by its Japanese name, *kaizen*. This is the belief that things are never perfect and could always be better. It is the acceptance that dramatic changes are unlikely to yield the best returns; relentless, incremental progress should be the objective.

As ever, all this is easy to say and hard to do. It takes genuine willpower and self-confidence – and those are rare qualities.

In many respects, managing a new business is much harder than running an established operation. In a new company there are no tried and tested systems, or department experts – everything has to be learned from scratch. Often this means the founder tries every task themselves – that way they understand the pitfalls, and how to do the job properly.

I spent a while in Belgo Centraal, one of London's largest restaurants serving 1,000 meals on a busy day, working in the pot wash. You only realize what a tough job it is when you have actually worked yourself in the heat and the steam as a *plongeur*.

An end to pygmy bosses and grey leaders

Shakespeare said, 'We cannot all be masters.' So some have to lead, and some must follow. But who is to take command? Many business schools believe they can give lessons in leadership. Others are advocates of executive coaching. I have doubts about such formal learning for something as elusive as leadership. You cannot study how to be the boss from a dusty text-book or in the lecture theatre: it is a skill that is either innate or acquired on the job.

Sadly, this is an age of pygmy bosses and grey lead-ers. Too few have real flair or a persona with a sense of high drama. The characters have been replaced by committees. Many twenty-first-century 'leaders' are simply administrators or over-promoted bureaucrats.

Where are the swashbucklers like Lord Hanson or Jimmy Goldsmith? Or the empire-builders like Joseph Lockwood at EMI, Lew Grade at ATV or Ernie Harrison at Racal?

Of course, chiefs do not *have* to be flamboyant to succeed. Stuart Williams, the co-founder of Topps Tiles (a former investment of mine), is a case study in mod-esty. And Sir John Rose at Rolls-Royce has enjoyed a low-profile but brilliant tenure as chief executive.

Unfortunately, the media tends to eviscerate any public figure who is anything other than well round-ed or fails to comply precisely with orthodox views. So functionaries take centre stage, too afraid to push through difficult policies, forever trying to accommo-date everyone.

That is not how great businesses are built. Great businesses are built by confident men and women who understand Goethe's maxim: 'Whatever you can do, or dream you can, begin it. Boldness has genius, power and magic in it. Begin it now.' Instead, companies are too often controlled not by titans of the boardroom, but by shadowy hedge-fund managers, faceless critics and corporate governance experts who have never run so much as a whelk stall.

'Great spirits
have always
found violent
opposition from
mediocrities'

Albert Einstein

Management gurus reckon one of the attributes of an outstanding leader is a **high** 'emotional quotient' – empathy for people. The principle makes sense, although the term sounds a bit awkward. Certainly, charm is helpful. But the most vital talent in leaders I've known is an ability to take decisions.

Staff like a boss who is decisive above all things, so they understand the direction of travel. Indeed, it can be better to take a bad decision and correct it later than procrastinate and sit on the fence.

Intellectuals rarely make great leaders because they over-complicate. If you are given the task of running things, you should remind yourself frequently: Simplify! Simplify!

Modern managers too often enjoy theory rather than doing things. A true leader has a bias for action, and a degree of impatience with the current order of things. And the best leaders possess great willpower, which tends to beat qualifications and sensitivity when it comes to getting things done.

They aren't usually highly technical types – but they know how to enthuse and inspire. Not for me the dull conformists who tick the right boxes, but have no hinterland or zest for life. I despair when I see how many companies are run by humourless number-crunchers. They understand finance and how to be prudent, but caution can never be the watchword for a fired-up workforce.

Ultimately, the finest leaders must be winners. They may get it right only 51 per cent of the time, but that can still lead to victory. The fact is that agile small companies can defeat big lumbering corporations. So often large firms focus more on internal politics than keeping their customers or staff happy. An owner contributes their zeal and personal touch, which can make a huge difference.

Like everyone, successful leaders need plenty of luck and good timing. With all their passion and ambition, high performers have an intuitive understanding of cycles and markets. They never let their audacity – or tenacity – drive them to ruin. They possess resilience to withstand the weasels who would happily see them fail. They boost morale; they have the energy to see the task through, and the sense to step aside before they grow complacent or corrupt.

Coping with talent

Anyone who employs talented people knows that talent is a rare commodity. The entrepreneur should move heaven and earth to hire it. Yet at the same time, no company should ever be in thrall to its stars.

It seems that in a number of industries, the entire enterprise appears to be directed towards enriching senior staff – while capital providers receive scant returns.

Take professional football clubs: managers and star players essentially take all the prizes, while shareholders almost invariably lose money. Stories of corporate insolvencies of soccer clubs are legion. I can recall an ex-owner of Everton telling me that buying it was the worst decision of his career. He not only lost money, but also had fans spit at him and hurl bricks through his sitting-room window. Football clubs are essentially charities run for the financial benefit of staff, as are most investment banks.

Often talent can bend companies to their will because of the myth that ideas are what create value. To repeat: execution is what matters.

Lots of people can imagine something original – a film, a song, a financial structure. Yet those concepts need investment and must be put into action and marketed. Almost all large undertakings are the work of hundreds of able bodies, all striving to deliver the goods. Intellectual capital is dispersed. Possibly top managers at banks, music companies, football clubs and suchlike allow themselves to be captured by wily operators. And many corporate executives implicitly link their pay and benefits to the escalating rewards seized by the 'special' talent. So this merry-go-round of excessive remuneration actually suits the custodians of shareholder wealth.

Traditional capital-intensive sectors like manufacturing are less prone to the 'winner-takes-all' disease. Western economies are scarily dependent on the sort of service industries where supposedly rare talent can hold companies to ransom.

Owners and executives have a duty to ignore such blackmail, and invest in young up-and-comers rather than greedy established players. There is plenty of brilliance out there, and lots of substitutes who can match the big names in the quality stakes (although many head-hunters would argue otherwise, because they too are on the gravy train).

No one is ever irreplaceable. It takes courage to confront the demands of an expensive safe bet and try someone new, but frequently it is worth the risk.

Astute use of performance-related pay and equity incentives is a key way to attract and retain the right people. You should be willing to dilute your ownership a little for the right recruits. Make sure you can claw back such instruments if the joiners leave too soon – shares and options should vest slowly.

Trouble within

It's a sad fact that if an entrepreneur employs enough people, sooner or later there will be a thief on the payroll. Most staff members are basically honest, but it's tedious and depressing to deal with the few who are not. Nevertheless, the aspiring entrepreneur should resolve to learn from every experience, and theft reveals a great deal about workplace psychology.

I learned a lesson about fiddling business expenses early in my career. In those days I knew a hard-bitten Australian mining promoter who regularly took over companies and then fired the management – usually without problems. He told me his technique: the day he bought the business he always went to the accounts department and examined in great detail every senior executive's expense forms to detect fiddles. It was a rare occasion when he didn't end up with enough incriminating material to sack whoever he wanted.

For some, padded expenses are normal practice – a

top-up to their salary. I suspect they help make the world of posh restaurants go round: some of the venues I once owned, such as The Ivy, derived at least a third of their overall income from business accounts. I wonder how many such meals are legitimate costs incurred in the course of work duties? But defrauding expenses is a perilous game with an ignominious history. You'll be all too familiar with the Westminster MPs' expenses scandal of 2009, but our Right Hon colleagues are not alone. Japan's agriculture minister Toshikatsu Matsuoka committed suicide after claiming almost £120,000 worth of utility fees at his parliamentary office – despite the fact such services are free in government offices. Tyco CEO Dennis Kozlowski awarded to himself and other executives hundreds of millions of dollars in unauthorized loans and gifts. The more he earned, the more he appropriated for himself in dubious deals. He ended up with a twenty-seven-year jail sentence.

Why is it that well-paid people rip off their employers? Generally it is not because they need the money. They do it because they feel exploited or hate their boss – or because they like the risk. It's the same thrill some people get from running off without paying a restaurant bill, even though they can afford it. Surveys suggest men often cheat their expenses to impress the opposite sex. Other research I've seen indicates as many as one in five workers does it. Apparently the culprits rarely feel guilty – perhaps because they only get caught occasionally.

One could say that at the base of Kozlowski's behaviour was a form of narcissism born of success.

Under Kozlowski, Tyco grew its market cap 7,000 per cent; perhaps that fostered a sense in Kozlowski that he and the company were one – and it's impossible to steal from oneself, no?

Regrettably, a misplaced sense of entitlement need not be restricted to big-time CEOs. It can occur in any role. I've mentioned that one of the first public companies I got involved with almost twenty years ago had accounts that overstated revenues and concealed liabilities – possibly because the finance director was senior partner at the auditors. I note Kozlowski trained as an auditor. To this day, I prefer modest and unassuming people in audit roles. Welcome to the world of high finance!

Other companies I've owned have suffered from ghost employees, forged cheques, faked robberies, organized credit-card scams, counterfeit banknotes, phoney refunds, payments to bogus suppliers, invoice kickbacks, staff working for competitors and hands straightforwardly in the till. I doubt my experiences are worse than average. If a theft or fraud can be carried out – it will be. Mostly the sums are not huge and the fraudsters tend to be amateurs. But the cons always disappoint – they involve lies, betrayal and other seedy behaviour that occasionally makes you despair of human nature.

Seasoned entrepreneurs end up more suspicious and cynical than beginners. We start out trusting people, and end up expecting assets to be misappropriated at every turn. This is why the security sector is so huge. Regrettably, you need to be constantly vigilant, especially in cash businesses like retailing or the restaurant trade. I hate euphemisms like 'shrinkage', used by shopkeepers to describe shoplifting costs. It makes it seem as if the offence is hardly a crime. Yet shoplifting costs businesses billions every year, despite retailers spending billions to tackle it. And this comes on top of employee thefts adding billions more to the total. It's not shrinkage: it's theft.

Private-life drama

Anyone who has ever had any management responsibilities will know that everyone's work is influenced by their private life. Vanni Treves, my predecessor as chairman of Channel 4, gave me advice on the subject. He said he understood the motivations and behaviour of executives much better if he was aware of the pertinent facts about their personal situation. His advice was sound. It should be part of the role of any boss to know the critical domestic circumstances of their juniors – so that they can help if a crisis erupts. It doesn't mean you should pry, but it does mean you should be acquainted with their hinterland.

I've mentioned that some years ago I was involved with a construction business where the chief executive's wife drank heavily. I had heard there were problems in their marriage but had no idea she was an alcoholic. Eventually the stress of his difficulties at home combined with the responsibilities of running a company overwhelmed him, and my colleague had a nervous breakdown. Inevitably this led to trouble at the company and a severely impaired investment. If I had been more aware of my ex-colleague's turmoil at home, I could have reacted more promptly to head off the looming disaster.

Tom Perkins, co-founder of the legendary venture capital firm Kleiner Perkins, tells a self-deprecating story in his excellent autobiography *Valley Boy* (Nicholas Brealey, 2008). He describes how he backed an entrepreneur with whom he had worked some years previously. Since he was familiar with this character, he didn't bother taking references. However, soon after getting funding, the entrepreneur started exhibiting signs of extreme paranoia. Eventually Perkins became concerned and did some background research. A horror story emerged. The entrepreneur was addicted to cocaine, and had already wrecked his family life and destroyed another business – as well as his nasal passages. Inevitably the business failed, after a saga involving death threats and embezzlement. Quite a price to pay for financing an entrepreneur you didn't know as well as you thought.

An entrepreneur receiving any sum of equity finance should know that the investors are morally and practically entitled to full disclosure about you. Kroll and similar corporate detectives are frequently hired to do detailed checks on managers in buyouts. Personally I always like to have a reasonable idea of someone's net worth if I'm supporting their business plan. I want to know if someone has significant borrowings or huge financial outgoings. Banks invariably request health check-ups as part of due diligence prior to granting debt facilities. These are a sensible insurance policy:

in one prospective deal I found out that the CEO of a business had a serious heart condition. That discovery threw the whole undertaking into chaos.

The most common personal issue I've encountered among associates has been the male mid-life crisis, with the classic accoutrements: mistress, motorbike, drugs, long hair, and even cosmetic surgery. The repercussions are usually bad. Deceit and intimations of mortality often combine in an explosive cocktail which then leads to divorce, distraction, depression and sometimes worse. I once offered a senior executive a six-month sabbatical if he would drop his plans to abandon his wife and four small children in order to live with his PA. But my gesture was rejected, and he proceeded to demolish his marriage and career.

Leaders do not need to be therapists to their staff, but a bit of amateur psychiatry does no harm. One of the best media managers I know says he spends all day just listening to his subordinates' woes. Once they have unburdened they leave his office feeling better. Since all companies are people businesses, sympathy, a decent emotional quotient and some humanity can go a long way in getting the best returns – both social and financial.

The necessary evil of HR

All too often, entrepreneurs think that their company isn't grown-up unless it has important-sounding head-office functions. The most egregious of these imagined needs is for a HR department. The very utterance of the letters HR should strike fear into the heart of every self-respecting entrepreneur.

In his 1977 book *Up the Organisation* (Jossey Bass, 2007), the brilliant Avis boss Robert Townsend (the man behind the legendary slogan 'We Try Harder') suggests the best thing to do is fire the entire personnel department. Indeed, I have radically downsized HR in several firms I've run, and business has gone all the better for it.

But tragically, we live in a time of overwhelming employment legislation, so getting legal procedures right can save a lot of time and heartache and that is the sort of task HR handles. They are probably the very definition of a necessary evil for a twenty-first-century business.

Human resources are like many parts of modern firms: they are a pure expense and a burden on the backs of the productive workers. Other divisions that can become the enemy include IT, legal and marketing. They don't sell and they don't produce: they consume. They are the amorphous support services. Often it makes sense to sub-contract these activities, and reward the external provider based on performance. If they don't deliver, you don't pay and you can replace them.

It is a grave error to give in to the pressure for departmental fiefdoms: effective leaders care about results, not process or turf.

Typically an apparatus builds up around divisions like HR to expand their role and cost more money. Compensation consultants are hired to come up with justifications for paying everyone more. Training advisors are employed to distract everyone from doing their job with pointless courses. Appraisal experts are contracted to critique staff relations. Experts are drafted in to devise an appropriate Corporate Social Responsibility Agenda – whatever that is.

All this paraphernalia is accepted as essential good practice by modern-thinking corporate management. Most of it is an expensive, bureaucratic load of hogwash.

Of course, senior executives understand that HR directors are powerful – a bit like Mossad or the CIA. Personnel know everyone's salary and bonus and all their disciplinary records. Wily office politicians cultivate them, since they help decide who gets a pay rise and promotion, how contracts are drafted, how individuals are treated if there's a restructuring and so on. Meanwhile head-hunters spend their time cultivating the top talent and shuffling the deck, profiting at every turn.

Perhaps it's fortunate that the bracing winds of a downturn often clear away a lot of pointless administration. Companies cut back on non-essential functions and ship expensive jobs abroad to cheap countries where they can. Legislators who have never met a payroll refuse to understand that when they gold-plate employment rights, they ultimately destroy jobs and prosperity. That is why unemployment is so high in countries like Spain.

Start-ups cannot really afford to take on a full-time HR person. Instead you might consider subscribing to one of the services that provides phone and online support, or perhaps hiring a part-time substitute.

Part 3
POINTS OF STYLE

Bring back the Renaissance men

I once attended a talk by an especially articulate chairman of a FTSE-100 public company. He made the telling comment that successful entrepreneurs were 'less interesting and less content than they were twenty-five years ago'. He also asserted that clinical depression among very high achievers in business was reaching epidemic proportions. I suspect this applies more to corporate officers than owner-managers, but it's still an arresting observation. Why should such high achievers be so miserable?

There is no doubt that owners and operators of large enterprises have a predisposition towards stress. They enjoy pressure and thrive on adrenaline and challenge. Inevitably, while a certain degree of anxiety is healthy, too much worry can lead to imbalance and unhappiness.

Today there is no escape from the grind: the intensity of global competition, the ubiquity of mobile phones, endless instant messaging and emails, and the pace of economic and technical change. High-powered leaders of industry are dealing in many time zones, at home as well as the office or factory, and find it harder to switch off than ever before. Despite lots of holidays, there is no relief from the worries of work, the striving for recognition and meeting budgets.

In years gone by, no one used the word 'workaholic'. It seemed most prosperous men of position enjoyed a leisurely, rounded existence. They contributed to the community, they went to church, and they had a close but large family. Nowadays we are not sure what the community is, few hold serious religious beliefs, and all too often the tycoon dumps the first wife for a trophy model. Relationships fray during the struggle. Bosses and the self-employed are prone to loneliness anyway – the dislocation and lack of intimacy in modern life can only serve to amplify this.

Expectations are much higher than they were in previous generations. Even though captains of industry have always known about those with more wealth, fame and power than they, now they are more likely to read and hear about them in more detail than ever before, thanks to vast quantities of 'success media'. Disappointment seems easy to come by, satisfaction hard to achieve. Too often, the restless, creative urge possessed by the ambitious can mutate into despondency and a sense of failure.

Should we really care if a few of the capitalist elite are gloomy and dull? I think it does matter: their decisions affect us all. If the successful business builders are narrow minded and neurotic, their staff suffer, their families suffer, their businesses suffer and possibly society as a whole suffers. Who is more likely to believe in the public good – the rapacious entrepreneur, or the ambitious person who also has a close family and a life outside work?

There are some answers to these problems.

We should revise our view that business leaders should be really obsessive about their work – passionate, by all means, but not pathological.

Equally harmful is the belief that everyone is good at only one thing: most people are multi-talented, and failure in one sphere should not preclude success in another. Intellectual variety helps relieve stress and boredom and can put compulsive competitiveness into context.

Sabbatical breaks strike me as a sound idea: an opportunity to contemplate and perhaps switch careers. The Renaissance figure, traditionally sneered at by specialists as a 'dilettante', might well be a more balanced performer and a more useful contributor.

Too much of business life involves sedentary activities like meetings and phone calls. Many doctors now prefer to prescribe exercise as a first treatment for patients complaining of depression. Physical exertion can be a tremendous release and is a pleasant contrast to the mental irritations of commerce. It is a more natural cure than drugs such as Prozac, and one that is often overlooked.

Becoming fit and feeling physically healthier can contribute positively to a general feeling of well-being. Stretching the mind and body is the way to better leaders and more exciting businesses, and is my first advice to any entrepreneur burning out from the struggle.

There always will be blood

There's a wonderful phrase by Joseph Conrad: 'To be a great autocrat you must be a great barbarian.' It sums up the theme of the brilliant film *There Will Be Blood*

(2007). The movie tells the tale of a monstrous oil prospector, who makes a fortune but destroys all those around him. To anyone curious about the dark side of the entrepreneurial dream, it is required viewing.

But is it true to life? Do successful business leaders need to be obsessive, friendless and brutal? Or can they be sensitive, balanced human beings?

I can certainly think of a few entrepreneur-savages, with Robert Maxwell being the best example I ever met. There was something menacing and hard-hearted about the man. He was an ingenious tyrant, who charmed and bullied all those around him and made and lost a massive publishing fortune while stealing hundreds of millions from his firm's pensioners.

He really was evil; I imagine that perhaps Beelzebub himself reached out from the watery depths, plucked Maxwell from the deck of his yacht *Lady Ghislaine* and spirited him off to hell. For Captain Bob had surely sold his soul to the devil many years before.

But the Bouncing Czech is not typical of the breed. Most wealth creators retain at least a veneer of civilized behaviour. Nevertheless, when cornered or roused to fury, they can be ruthless. In 1853, the shipping and railroad magnate Cornelius Vanderbilt wrote to two former business associates, Morgan and Garrison: 'You have undertaken to cheat me. I won't sue you, for the law is too slow. I'll ruin you.' He then proceeded to make good on his promise.

The modern-day autocrats are surely the Russian oligarchs. They looted their nation's assets in an orgy of corruption under the drunken President Boris Yeltsin. It is inconceivable that so few amassed so much through strictly legal means. The result is a disastrous concentration of wealth and influence, and a deeply divided society. It is hard to feel sorry for those who have since been stripped of their empires, although history may yet show Putin and his successor to have been even worse custodians of the nation's resources.

Many ambitious men in business carry grudges and almost relish feuds. Inevitably the battles are over money and power.

Someone who clearly loves a punch-up is Sumner Redstone, the media mogul who controls Viacom and CBS. He had a protracted and public falling-out with his own daughter Shari, who was destined to take over the $40-billion entertainment empire on Redstone's death (an event which he was still insisting was a long way off – at the age of eighty-seven). His son Brent and nephew Michael have both sued him over disputed share sales. On top of this Redstone famously fell out with Tom Cruise, perhaps the biggest star at his movie studio Paramount. He had this to say about the value of a showdown: 'Confrontation leads to the truth.'

As you claw your way to the top of the capitalist heap, the struggle can blunt your senses. All too often self-made men have come up the hard way, and they continue to see existence as survival of the fittest long after they attain material security.

Commercial success is about endless tough decisions – getting out of messy situations that haven't worked, beating the competition, running a low-cost operation and so forth.

But sometimes the oxygen in the boardroom can get mighty thin, and bosses lose perspective. Partners, family, and friends can get sacrificed for another deal, another dollar. The competitive spirit, once unleashed, is a primitive urge that can wreak havoc.

The decent-minded go-getter keeps it under control, and thus remains a master of his soul. That means retaining balance, perhaps over a chat with a mentor or your spouse, keeping your business and career in perspective, and trying hard not to bring work troubles home.

Fatherhood and the entrepreneur

The life of a self-made man is not always pleasant. Driving hard bargains, dealing with litigation, juggling creditors, making staff redundant, fighting for customers – these are all part of the craft of running your own show. Managing a business can have a brutalizing influence on your character. But becoming a father has a healthy, humanizing impact, putting all the stress and ambition into perspective.

The favourite small talk in the twenty-first century among entrepreneurs is not football – thank God – but discussing one's family. It is a civilized contrast to all that wealth accumulation. This is the first generation of New Man executives whose chief hobbies are their children rather than golf and drinking. These leaders can not only close a sale or raise venture capital; they can change a nappy, babysit and talk about exams.

This is a huge change from the 1960s and 70s. The old male boss delegated all child-rearing to his wife or the nanny. He was rarely there for carol concerts or parent evenings, or sometimes even for the birth! He was too busy building a fortune, and in the evenings socializing with work clients or bankers. But nowadays bosses can be seen slipping out of the office early to be home in time for the children's bath and a bedtime story. There is a little stab of guilt when I do it – but I think it's worth it.

Will we make better dads? I hope so. Will it compromise our careers and stunt our material success? Will our children thank us for the extra attention? Who knows?

I've been fortunate in having children relatively late, so I am less obsessed by the struggle for advancement than I was in my twenties and thirties. Then I had no responsibility to provide for others; if I failed I was the loser, but no one else suffered. But those who marry and have children young face tougher choices. Do they go all-out for success and perhaps miss their children growing up? Because it's pretty hard to get ahead if you're only willing to do short days and never work at weekends. And the burden of school fees and suchlike can be hell if you're also funding a start-up.

I have met plenty of alpha males who have achieved great things, but sacrificed their personal lives along the way. Often they divorced because they were never at home. Sadly material success tends to come at an emotional price. Interestingly, from the domestic debris they mostly seem to forge close relationships with their children once they are grown up. Or they have subsequent marriages and bond better with their children at the second attempt.

I was lucky in that my dad taught me by example to make my own way in the world and believe anything is possible. It is sad that so many captains of industry have a single overwhelming regret: that their father never lived to see them become the conquering hero. After all, logic would indicate entrepreneurs and children should get on well, since they are similar in many ways: impatient, self-centred, demanding, enthusiastic, energetic, and wilful. Occasionally at board meetings it can be difficult to tell them apart; but perhaps that is what makes them fun to have around.

Some day my prince will come (home early)

What do you need to marry an entrepreneur? Looks? Wealth? Intelligence? Perhaps all three – but more than anything you should possess the virtue of tolerance.

By their nature empire builders are obsessives who focus on their careers relentlessly. They feel they have a mission to create. And something in life usually has to give. That means a partner must be accommodating: willing to sacrifice almost everything for the business – and willing to put up with the ego of their ambitious other half. Moreover, most entrepreneurs I've worked with are never satisfied: 'just enough' is not a concept that appeals to them. So all too often, once a target has been met, huge new challenges are set. This can take its toll on a relationship, and I suspect entrepreneurs have a higher divorce rate than average.

Of course, this lust for glory is part of their make-up and, to some, of their appeal in the first place. No one marries an entrepreneur expecting him or her to be a pushover. But someone who is boss of all they survey can carry on barking out orders even when they get home. Hugely successful entrepreneurs probably don't make for tranquil life companions as a rule.

Sometimes business owners partner with their spouse to grow a company. There is even a word for them – 'copreneurs'. Gordon and Anita Roddick of The Body Shop were the classic example. Often a married couple can make a formidable team: living and working together, dreaming and striving night and day to develop an enterprise. This combination means bringing up a family can be quite a strain, but the self-employed tend to have high levels of energy and are good at coping. Another interesting set-up is where each partner is an entrepreneur but they run different firms – for instance, Christian Rucker of The White Company and her husband Nick Wheeler of Charles Tyrwhitt. They also have four children: life must be fairly hectic in their home. At least such partners know how entrepreneurs think and behave.

For some entrepreneurs it makes sense to marry later. By that time they have achieved a certain amount of material success, and are probably searching for more balance in their lives. There is less pressure to work 100-hour weeks and prove themselves to the world. I know one mightily successful financial services entrepreneur who settled down and had two children in his late forties, and now concentrates on travel, yoga and growing trees. He still competes, but since he made a fortune by the age of forty, money is no longer the principal objective.

Entrepreneurs can have unrealistic expectations of their personal life. Their self-confidence can be so overpowering that they see their domestic situation as an extension of the office. They might want a partner to stimulate them intellectually – but they probably also want someone to organize a home, social life and family. They want a supportive listener who lets them make decisions – but they also like to be impressed. This can lead to mismatches and dashed expectations. Certain entrepreneurs deliberately marry achievers from a different sphere – the arts, public service, media – because they want an equal but not a competitor.

Inevitably there is no remarkable formula that leads to happiness and an enduring relationship. Human emotions mean that someone who is only ever rational in commercial affairs can still be blind in love. Somehow that trait is more endearing than the idea of a money-making machine who cannot even get carried away in affairs of the heart.

The delights of the portfolio career

I once attended a dinner party where the host went round the table one by one, describing what each of us did for a living. It was a sobering moment. Here were our lives, summed up in a few words. Is this really how we will be remembered? Is this all we have done?

Ever since Adam Smith published *The Wealth of Nations* in 1776, modern societies have focused on the division of labour. It is one of the platforms on which industrial capitalism is constructed. We have become ever more specialist in our work – no one wants to be known as a jack of all trades, master of none. Today it is all niches. After all, the sum of human knowledge has expanded exponentially since Leonardo da Vinci's day, when the concept of a Renaissance man, who had learning across all fields, was valid. Now someone like that would be dismissed as a dilettante.

Yet this narrowing of interest and expertise is not entirely a good thing. For example, the rise and rise of the life-long, professional politician has been bad for government and democracy; too many politicians now enter government never having held a real job. They lack exposure to other perspectives, other worlds. And they spend far too long in power once they get a seat.

There should be term limits at all levels in public appointments. At Channel 4 I was allotted a maximum of six years in the job to make an impact, before

I was to move on and give someone fresh a go – and before I got bored and boring too. This sort of churn in our institutions is healthy: it allows new talent to rise to the top, and stops office-holders from becoming complacent and a blockage to progress.

And ultimately there must be more to our lives than one constricting discipline. We have so much more time on earth than in the fifteenth century: our careers can now last fifty years or more. I studied medicine partly because I thought doctors can have a varied existence: not only do they treat patients – they can also do research, teach, write, administrate and even run health-care companies. We do not all have to be polymaths, but surely the prejudice against people who do more than one thing is wrong.

When I became chairman of Channel 4 there was criticism that I was a novice in the media world. Yet one of the problems of broadcasting management is that it is insular, with participant firms historically cut off thanks to scarce spectrum. But with the infinite bandwidth of the Internet, traditional media companies are being leapfrogged by upstarts like Google – newcomers without the arrogance and tunnel vision of the specialists.

Surely none of us really wants to be pigeon-holed. It is nice to have a title and profession – 'lawyer', 'chef', 'programmer' and so on – but don't we all have the capacity to do more than one sort of work over the course of decades?

We each have many talents. Climbing to the top of the hierarchy in many organizations means long service and, most likely, focus on one discipline in one sector. Our system means the ambitious may be frightened to diversify if they want to seize the glittering prizes. Yet jobs for life and final-salary pension schemes are twentieth-century relics, now gone. The future belongs to those who plan a series of consecutive careers, or perhaps simultaneous roles – either part-time or even moonlighting.

I accept that the concept of the all-conquering generalist manager is flawed. You need contacts and understanding, which tend to come with years of dedication to a single vocation.

But those who consciously choose to keep things fresh are qualitatively different from those who are generalists by accident. One inspires admiration, the other suspicion.

Even those with particular skills and qualifications can lead a portfolio life to a degree. Most of us have multiple existences – family, hobbies, home. It is oppressive and inefficient to be trapped too much by corporate ritual and tradition. A chief executive I know has on his card the designation 'Founder', an attractively broad category, and I know another businessman friend who calls himself an impresario – again, a usefully adaptable word.

Centuries ago there were no sharp divisions between the state and private sector, between science and the arts. Bring back that enlightened approach! We should shrug off attempts to keep everyone labelled, and encourage life-long learning and successive occupations across different callings. Long live *Homo universalis*!

The mythical entrepreneur

There are a lot of misconceptions about those who build companies.

These fictions are unhelpful because they discourage some would-be entrepreneurs from giving it a go, and even influence policy makers in their decisions. So I thought it would be worthwhile debunking some of the common falsehoods.

O **Entrepreneurs are mainly motivated by money:** In reality, they create firms by accident, or because they want to prove themselves, or because they are bored, or have a passion. Obviously some want to get rich, but wealth is rarely the sole point of the exercise. Studies have shown that the short phrase which best sums up the drive of those who create new enterprises is 'I'll show them.' Money is a way of keeping the score and providing capital for the next project.

O **The idea is what matters:** In fact, execution is everything. We all have brilliant concepts which will never come to fruition because they are impractical, or because we are too lazy or distracted. Making it happen is what really counts, and this is the difficult bit – which is why so many seemingly clever schemes fail.

O **Entrepreneurs are born, not made:** Research shows that most successful business owners do not start out very young. They gain experience working

for others, and learn how to run an enterprise before venturing out on their own. Just as no one is
genetically programmed to be a doctor or an architect, so entrepreneurs tend to find their calling by
nurture rather than nature.

O **Start-ups are one-man bands:** Most firms that do
well are developed by teams rather than by a single
man or woman. There may be a prime mover who
gets most of the attention – and possibly the rewards – but it is the winning combination of skills
formed by a *partnership* of players that is the most
likely formula for success.

O **Entrepreneurs are inventive geniuses:** Very few
true inventors make it big in business. Rather, it
is the commercially minded individual who repli-
cates an original product and makes it cheaper, or
markets it better, or watches the costs properly – or
simply gets lucky with his timing – who tends to
strike gold.

O **Entrepreneurs are mostly academic rejects with
no qualifications:** In fact, more and more business
owners have university degrees – or even doctorates. These days many MBA students end up running their own companies. Being an entrepreneur
has become a respectable career choice, so more of
the educated middle class has taken the plunge.

O **Most new businesses fail:** Actually, the survival
rates for companies have been rising in recent years.
Only a small proportion of operating enterprises go
bust each year, as opposed to inactive companies

being wound up or struck off, which distorts the statistics. And firms usually fail because of management shortcomings, rather than external forces.

O **Entrepreneurs are loners:** It takes people skills to grow a company, and most entrepreneurs are extroverts who enjoy the company of others, not introverts. They choose to work for themselves because they enjoy the freedom and independence, not because they want to hide away from colleagues.

O **Entrepreneurs are gamblers:** Yes they take financial risks, but most entrepreneurs are good at judging the downside, and are more cautious in their ventures than it might appear to the uninformed. The vast majority of bankrupts are not entrepreneurs who failed: they are salaried people who borrowed too much.

O **Entrepreneurs are workaholics:** This is certainly no myth at the start of the entrepreneur's journey, when a founder needs to be committed. But at a certain point, most business proprietors work no more hours than ambitious corporate managers – and at least the self-employed can choose their own work patterns. Moreover, surveys show the most stressful aspects of life for staff in big companies are office politics and commuting, things entrepreneurs can largely avoid.

My list suggests that running your own show is neither as difficult nor as miserable as many people think.

What's stopping you?

Ritualism in business

I often hear entrepreneurs complain of how much tougher commercial conditions are than they used to be, and how much more competitive markets are these days.

In reality, contemporary entrepreneurs enjoy almost idyllic circumstances compared to their predecessors. We have inherited centuries of technical and social progress. Massive leaps in productivity and vast accumulated knowledge mean virtually everything at work is quicker, easier and more comfortable. Despite much brave talk of how overworked all of us are, in truth an entrepreneur's day is occasionally spent devising ways of filling time so that they can feel important.

Take, for example, conferences and seminars. These are for the most part a waste of time: in general they achieve no underlying business purpose. During the talks half the audience falls asleep; the only memorable part of the speech will be the jokes; and the audio-visual effects usually go wrong. Often all the speakers do is read their dull script in a lifeless monotone. At the end few can even be bothered to ask any questions.

The entire affair is a sort of farce, except that firms spend many thousands of pounds a year sending their staff to these ludicrous events. Trade shows can be similar nonsense; just an excuse for a booze-up.

However, they get people out of the office and involve free food and drink, and companies can say they spend large sums of money on training, which is meant to be a sensible investment in people. The point about such silly occasions is that they have become part of the ritual of being in business – one of the devices aimed at keeping us all 'doing something', so that we can all justify our next bonus and say how busy we are when asked.

In the very early days of any business, I would say avoid conferences, seminars and trade shows entirely – they absorb money and time. Later on you can attend a few, as long as you are ruthlessly discriminating about which ones you choose.

Another less formal mechanism for keeping people occupied in the workplace is office politics. This phenomenon has been around a long time, but has better chances to flourish when there is less real work to do. In a bizarre way it can take hold best in big, fat organizations where everything is humming along nicely and all the serious stuff is taken care of. In small, start-up companies which lurch in and out of crisis – as they always do – the ever-present risk of a visit from the bailiffs discourages the decadence of office politics in favour of survival.

The greatest ritual of all is, of course, the 'meeting'.

This is a magnificent engine of bullshit of all kinds. It gives the participants the feeling they are making progress with their project, whatever it may be.

Meetings range from inter-departmental to board to annual general. One of the most accomplished capitalists I ever knew refused to meet almost anyone. He dealt with things with absolute expediency by telephone, and did not feel the desire to gather lots of men in suits in a posh room to discuss agendas, targets and mission statements, and then circulate minutes (another ritual of mind-boggling tedium) of the time wasted. I would guess **that** only 20 per cent of most board meetings are worthwhile – I'm sure if they were restricted to half an hour we would all enjoy life more.

Many rituals of business are being massively legitimized by the corporate governance movement, which is moving to ever more bizarre extremes – such as the idea once espoused by the Institute of Directors **th**at its members should sit examinations and gain qualifications to prove their fitness to manage.

Business is about successfully dealing with the marketplace, not attending a series of academic lectures. But quangos and bureaucrats live and breathe pointless rituals of all kinds, so one should not be surprised.

Start-ups do not have to fit in with the elaborate charade that comprises so much of corporate life. Freelancers can cut to the chase and dispense with the formalities that absorb so much time and energy. It is a huge competitive advantage – and makes the whole affair so much more exhilarating.

Made not born

I've argued that entrepreneurs are the product of nurture rather than nature; that environment more than inheritance shapes them. After all, is anyone *really* endowed with a God-given gift to build companies and make money? My observations over the decades suggest these skills are acquired through practical experience, rather than the right parentage. But I was occasioned to question my own belief by reading *Born, Not Made*, a book by leadership writers James Fisher and James Koch (Greenwood Press, 2008). It reasons that a substantial proportion of entrepreneurial behaviour is genetically determined.

The core of their argument is that entrepreneurs are a different breed who possess distinctive personalities, attitudes, values and habits. These individuals have an 'enterprise gene', if you like. Using recent evidence from behavioural genetics, they say the key traits of entrepreneurs – self-confidence, extroversion, high levels of energy, and a willingness to embrace risk – are all highly influenced by heredity.

This debate about what makes us who we are has carried on since Darwin put forward his theory of evolution in 1859. No doubt our DNA has an influence on the course of our life, but the very idea that all our actions and thoughts are predetermined is nonsense.

Someone who believes the opposite of *Born, Not Made* is Geoff Colvin, author of *Talent Is Overrated* (Nicholas Brealey, 2008). This book essentially argues that hard work pays. You won't be surprised to learn I agree with Colvin, and not Fisher and Koch.

Almost every high achiever I have dealt with has got there through graft rather than some miracle endowment of brains. A few appear to have greatness in the blood, yes, but more often than not I think they learn at their parents' feet as opposed to doing well thanks to innate advantages. I see entrepreneurs inspired by their mum and dad's efforts at self-employment.

Colvin gets support from *Outliers*, written by Malcolm Gladwell (Penguin, 2009), who suggests that you need to put 10,000 hours of work into your chosen arena to outperform. One wonders how he can be so precise, but I agree with the gist.

Gladwell also makes the point that circumstances and timing are crucial in deciding how glorious your career is. He notes that of a *Fortune* list of the seventy-five richest people of all time, fourteen are Americans born within nine years of each other in the mid-nineteenth century. By the time they were in their thirties and forties, the US was undergoing a massive industrial transformation – railroads, steel, manufacturing – and the opportunities were remarkable for those in that place at that time.

It's debatable whether there is a good or bad time to start a business, but there is a tremendous psychological fillip to be had from going solo, irrespective of the economic cycle.

When I left Kleinwort Benson in 1987, I felt an invigorating sense of independence, and unleashing of energy. A big employer might offer security and benefits, but what about creative satisfaction, what about the chance to live your dreams and change the world?

And so I believe fervently that we can all achieve something bold and enterprising with application, and luck. I absolutely reject the idea of *Born, Not Made*. Even in terrible economic conditions, I think if someone puts enough effort in, they might just make it.

After all, if inborn talent were all that determined

'It is better for a man to go wrong in freedom than to go right in chains'

Thomas Huxley

who climbed to the top of the heap, then why would ambitious sorts who lack conspicuous natural skills even bother? Society *needs* to believe that we can all better ourselves. That is the story of human progress.

The brogue element

Terry Smith, the UK financial stalwart and author of the bestseller *Accounting for Growth* (Random House, 1996), once told me about his footwear test of investment analysis: back the captain of industry who wears practical shoes with plastic soles, rather than the one who wears ultra-posh brogues from Church's, the UK shoemaker to olde-world City gents. The former captain will actually visit factories to find out what's going on; the latter is unlikely to be found outside London's West End. Do not be fooled by a clipped accent and a confident manner, or indeed packaging of any sort.

An ex-management consultant who had gone into the health-food industry once visited me. He had no experience of running a company, but that didn't put him off. He had raised significant funding for his start-up concept and had rolled out a number of branches. But despite a very slick business plan, it was apparent to me after half an hour that the economics of his retail model were fundamentally flawed. Clearly his backers were wowed by his trendy proposition, and forgot to verify the basics. Sadly, his company went bust in short order.

He was a classic example of the Counter-Presentational Principle, a theory of Richard Oldfield's propounded in his excellent investment book *Simple But Not Easy* (Doddington, 2007). The theory states that the ability of managers to do their job may be in inverse relationship to their ability to present well at meetings. In other words: just because an entrepreneur has produced a glossy document and possesses a fluent sales pitch, it does not necessarily follow that they will make investors money.

In a sense this is merely a variation on the ancient maxim: beware form over substance; which means, look at the underlying reality rather than the surface appearance of things. Like most such aphorisms, putting it into action takes work. We live in a visual age, when too often the superficial triumphs over the profound; but falling for the trivial rather than the serious can be deadly in enterprise.

This can be applied to many aspects of commercial life, not just the appraisal of business plans.

In interviews, I find it pays to probe beyond the smart suit, prepared CV and scripted answers, and get a real feel for the individual and their true capabilities. Taking genuinely independent references is essential.

Finance has always been naturally susceptible to the ebb and flow of fashion; perhaps even more than the rag trade. Companies and investors will rush towards the latest fad, as moths to a candle; that is how bubbles are created. Exponential growth is always the magic ingredient, be it the dotcom boom, China or alternative energy.

Of course, some of these new fads will turn out

'Do your thing and I shall know you'

Ralph Waldo Emerson

to be genuine opportunities, but that does not mean that *you* can make money out of them, especially if promoters have intermediated matters and taken the best profits.

So if you are picking a business partner, hiring a head of sales, or choosing a franchise formula – dig beneath the surface. Do not be taken in by froth – ask the tough questions, and be honest with yourself. Does the idea have staying power? Does your prospective partner get his or her hands dirty?

From time to time we all get seduced by ever-upwards projections of sales and profits. But few undertakings actually meet their founders' bullish expectations. Life has a tendency to interrupt. So many of us believe we are better at predicting the future than we really are.

I conclude once more that it's best to stick with variations of known formulas, rather than extraordinary promises that all too often are fantasies.

Part 4
THE CAPITAL PURSUIT

Tales of the Money Riverbank

'Go where the rich and powerful are,' I'd tell him, 'and learn their ways. They can be flattered and they can be scared. Please them enormously or scare them enormously, and one moonless night they will put their fingers to their lips, warning you not to make a sound. And they will lead you through the dark to the widest, deepest river of wealth ever known to man. You'll be shown your place on the riverbank, and handed a bucket all your own'
From Kurt Vonnegut's *God Bless You, Mr Rosewater*

Kurt Vonnegut might be unlikely inspiration for an entrepreneur, but he was right about at least one thing: the Money River really is out there, for those who would only stand in it.

The most common excuse I hear from those who want to start a business but haven't had the courage is that they can't raise the money. In my opinion, any project worthy of support will always get the necessary backing in the end. Whether the economy is up or down, the world is always awash with capital looking for exciting returns. However, every entrepreneur needs persistence and a decent business plan: as Matthew 7:7 says: 'Ask, and it shall be given you; seek and ye shall find; knock, and it shall be opened to you.'

Fortunately, there have never been more doors on which to knock. Since the advent of professional venture capital in the 1940s, the ecosystem for backing entrepreneurs has grown to the point where the options are almost bewildering.

In the search for funding, don't believe that any source of funding will suffice so long as there's enough money on offer. Investors differ markedly, and the entrepreneur must familiarize themselves with the various breeds.

The best-known investors are venture capitalists (VCs), angel investors and private equity. They might seem to blur together at the edges of each category, since they live side-by-side on a fairly seamless continuum, but they all differ.

Some angel investors are so rich and so formal in their approach that they resemble VCs, while some VCs behave like nightclub DJs. You'll soon have a sense of which one is right for you, and if you don't, they'll soon put you straight – usually by not returning your calls.

But let's start by considering the very best investor of them all: you.

Moonlighting: the best launch for a start-up

Occasionally, prospective entrepreneurs ask me whether they should quit their job to start a business or do it part-time while keeping their current job. I usually suggest the latter strategy, because it worked for me. For six years after university, I was employed by other people while moonlighting on my own projects, such as pubs and software companies, in the evenings, during weekends and holidays. I didn't take many holidays in my twenties, as I was too busy managing various ventures on the side.

The turning point came when a memo was circulated at Kleinwort Benson where I worked, stating that staff were not permitted to hold directorships or shareholdings in external companies. I knew then the time had come to take the plunge and embrace full-blown self-employment, so I jumped ship the following month and became independent. My sense of freedom was palpable, but I didn't regret the years juggling employment and entrepreneurship. It was part of my apprenticeship.

You will be tempted to think it can't be done, that you're just too tired when you get home from work or that there simply aren't enough hours in the day.

Doubtless you *will* be tired, and you *will* work long hours, but neither need be fatal.

A more pernicious excuse is that you happen to be interested in the kind of business that doesn't lend itself to out-of-hours working, in which case you might like to consult Emma Jones's book *Working 5 to 9: How to start a successful business in your spare time* (Harriman House, 2010), which profiles entrepreneurs who manage to combine day jobs with night-time businesses. It's a light and cheerful read, but still useful for anyone who thinks it's impossible to moonlight in their chosen sector. Jones interviews entrepreneurs who have managed to make a go of moonlighting in just about every sector – even pig farming. Reportedly office-supplies giant Staples sees a sharp spike in sales between 5 p.m. and 9 p.m., which the company attributes to '5 to 9ers' stocking up on the commute home for their after-hours endeavours.

The advantages of holding down a job while plotting to become an entrepreneur are plain. You receive an income to fund your secret project and pay the overheads while it develops; you learn your trade at someone else's expense; and you hedge your bets in case your freelance activities fizzle out.

Perhaps best of all, if your business takes off using your own funds then you will own all of it. You won't have to give away a dispiritingly large chunk of your earning potential to equity-hungry investors – indeed, some successful entrepreneurs consider the total retention of ownership to be key in building their fortune. Also, if you hang on to 100 per cent ownership then you won't be pressured to run the business according to the whims of investors. I prefer to buy businesses that don't need too much meddling – but other investors make a virtue of interfering.

The disadvantages of moonlighting are also clear: if you get caught by your boss misusing resources or getting distracted from the day job, there will be trouble; and a business run in your spare time will never receive the focus and devotion it needs to be truly successful.

If you are ambitious, the part-time option should only ever be temporary. To avoid being forever in stealth mode, you should have a 'boat-burning' target: a clearly defined point at which you chuck the day job and dive in. Don't tweak your fledgling business until it seems like a sure-fire bet: it never will be. It's very easy to tinker away on the margins for ever but, as Steve Jobs once said to a perfectionist engineer at Apple, 'real artists ship'.

The online revolution has made moonlighting easier than ever. As long as there is no conflict with your principal job, why shouldn't such an arrangement be successful? Of course, a part-time enterprise will have to become your hobby and consume your holidays. You must steel yourself for the prospect of 100-hour working weeks. It will test your determination: if you don't have the energy and commitment to put that effort in, don't expect the journey to get easier if you go full-time.

Frequently, such part-time enterprises are family affairs: the principal wage-earner remains in the day job, with its health, retirement and fringe benefits, while their partner runs the home business.

Certain ventures suit moonlighting: e-commerce, direct marketing, franchises, property and suchlike. The rise of virtual businesses has made part-time pursuits much easier to grow, thanks to the expansion of outsourcing. Of course, not everyone running a business alongside their main job wants to build an empire – some just enjoy the variety, freedom and extra income. You wouldn't be the only one. I've read about a survey of UK police forces showing that in one regional force alone, one in thirteen police officers had a second income. Some were tattoo artists. One was a horse dentist and another provided a holistic massage service. The most common sideline for these moonlighting cops was letting property or running a bed-and-breakfast. All are permitted, as long as they do not interfere with policing. I applaud the police authorities for taking such an enlightened view.

The biggest single hurdle for many start-ups is the proprietor's low or non-existent income in the early years. Is the sacrifice of a safe salary for the uncertainty of self-employment worth it for you? Will your family support you – emotionally, if not financially?

Multimillionaire Felix Dennis has a theory that children under a certain age have no view whatsoever about how rich their parents are: they only need to know that their parents love them. He might be right, but I imagine not every spouse is quite as black and white about it.

What often kills an early-stage business is excessive personal drawing of money by the owner, draining the company of vital working capital. This tends to happen when the founder has no understanding of finance, or indeed discipline about money. In the early years, very few start-ups can afford to provide the owner with a lavish lifestyle. Thinking otherwise is likely to be a delusion.

As ever, all these decisions come down to your personal philosophy. As Goethe said: 'Most people work the greater part of their time for a mere living.' Do you want that phrase to apply to you, or do you want to break out and at least try to make a difference?

If you moonlight, the downsides are reduced. It is the sensible compromise for many would-be entrepreneurs. Even if it means 100-hour weeks, it's likely that your employer's salary will be the least demanding investment capital you'll ever receive – followed by angel capital.

Summoning an angel

Angel investors are wealthy individuals who punt their own money in fledgling companies, and their contribution is routinely understated. A start-up entrepreneur is far more likely to get backing from an angel investor than from a venture capitalist, bank loan or government grant. That's partly because angels are more nimble and risk-positive than large institutions, and partly because they tend to make smaller investments, usually earlier on in the life of the company. Their money is easier to come by, and perhaps has slightly fewer strings attached.

Angel capital has been responsible for many great investments, from the start-up of Body Shop to the founding of the Ford Motor Company and the building of the Golden Gate Bridge in San Francisco in the 1930s. Backing risky undertakings is dangerous stuff, but the availability of this type of finance is crucial since commercial banks want collateral and, as we shall see, formal venture capital usually wants to back novel businesses in potentially huge markets. Don't ask a VC to help you open your first cafe. (If you own a profitable chain of 250 cafes and want to sell it then you might call on private equity investors, who buy and sell businesses with established cash flow, but that's another book).

Angels are sometimes characterized as 'amateur' investors, in the kinder sense of the word 'amateur', reflecting as it does the angel's solo status and not their competence or dedication. Likewise, VCs and private equity are often referred to as 'professional' investors, even if some are anything but.

The ways in which business angels invest differ markedly from the methods used by VCs and private equity. Business angels are essentially entrepreneurial-manager types, most of them having worked in small companies, with perhaps 80 per cent of them having started a small firm as an entrepreneur. By contrast, many private-equity executives are accountants, who fit the financial investor mould, and rather too many VCs are MBA types. Few of the professionals offer genuine hands-on help to small firms, whereas business angels frequently look for investments where they can add value in an active way.

Business angels focus less upon the financial rewards than the professionals. They expect lower rates of return and do much less stringent due diligence – an area where angels admit they are weak. Angels are much easier-going about getting involved with other investors, too. They tend not to charge fees when they invest, and are more likely to inject pure cash rather than saddle a company with complicated debt-style instruments, where investors might have borrowed money to buy your business. In such cases, it'll be down to your cash flow to pay off your investor's loan – or have the banks assume technical ownership and control of your business. It happens more often than one might think.

Angels make decisions much more quickly than VC firms, and are less concerned with a pre-planned exit than venture capitalists. Interestingly, business angels have backed far fewer high technology start-ups as a proportion of their overall early-stage deals than VC firms.

Both business angels and venture capitalists stress the importance of management. The enthusiasm, trustworthiness, track record and expertise of the entrepreneur(s) are rated as hugely significant investment criteria by each camp.

Business angels are the unsung heroes of the financial world, taking huge risks to get companies started and rolling their sleeves up to participate. Inevitably the angel ecosystem is far more developed in the USA, with some estimates putting the number at 250,000 angels investing tens of billions of dollars a year in thousands of growing businesses. I suspect as business angel investing becomes more sophisticated and organized, so the amounts invested by this group in the UK will expand. It couldn't happen soon enough: if I were twenty-five with no ties I'd relocate to Silicon Valley or New York in a flash, the better to draw upon the bountiful and sophisticated investor culture in those places.

So how do you reach this audience to raise equity? Despite the scale of business angel activity, it is an inefficient market. Both entrepreneurs and business angels complain that they find it difficult to meet each other and network effectively, but finding angel networks isn't difficult – a quick web search will reveal that every country has multiple trade organizations for angel investors.

It's worth noting at this stage that the race for funding is like every other appealing prize: it attracts a small percentage of scammers, incompetents and shady types. The hard part is working out which of the networks of angels offer legitimate benefits.

Some of these networks will ask you to part with your money, usually in return for details of your business plan being sent to a mailing list of angels or the chance to pitch to angels in person. So should an entrepreneur ever pay to pitch?

It's difficult to answer satisfactorily when angel investing is necessarily replete with broken dreams. One angel network, Angelsoft, reported in 2008 that only 1 per cent of its several thousand applicants received funding that year, with a further 10 per cent getting as far as due diligence.

Before paying for the chance to mix with angels, entrepreneurs should make their peace with the fact that even the most honest and effective angel networks generate thousands of disappointed prospectors every year, entirely legitimately. Thus if you make a pitch and no one bites, you've not necessarily been ripped off. It's far more likely that you didn't make the grade – this time, at least.

But with so many angel networks on offer you'll need to do some filtering of your own. You might start by looking at pedigree. It soon becomes apparent that some angel networks are run by people with no obvious record of great success themselves. Again, that's not evidence of a scam, but you could do worse than consider only those networks run by conspicuously high-achieving entrepreneurs, preferably serial entrepreneurs. Their honesty is to some extent certified by having built several successful businesses, whereas most fraudsters are obliged to maintain a low profile and continually move on.

I invested in a UK angel network (Beer and Partners) precisely because it is staffed by industry stalwarts I know and trust. The founders could show a long commitment to the cause, whereas the more fly-by-night networks are often as freshly minted as their business cards. Most pay-to-pitch networks are honest, though some are more effective than others.

Still, some commentators are vehemently against paying to pitch. They say that only bad ideas need to chase money, and that the smart money chases good ideas. This 'better mousetrap' argument is persuasive at first, but consider the lot of the angel investor: they're often inundated by dreamers seeking money for hopeless causes. If you've ever watched *American Inventor* or *Dragon's Den*, you'll know that the world is full of determined but misguided people who won't take no for an answer. It might be funny on TV, but it's not so funny when they're calling your PA asking for an appointment. It helps to have a filter, and pay-to-pitch angel networks deter the more trivial applications.

Perhaps the best argument against paying to pitch is simply that in some cases the fees are a significant proportion of the founders' seed capital: the money might have been better deployed in building the business. It's hard to object to that – but it all depends on the amount in question. Certainly, entrepreneurs should not exhaust their working capital to join an angel network.

There is a fantastic US book called *Finding Your Wings: How to locate private investors to fund your venture* by Gerald Benjamin and Joel Margulis (John Wiley, 1996). It provides detailed instructions on such matters as preparing an investor-oriented business plan and deciding whether you are dealing with 'a Deep-Pocket Investor, a Socially Responsible Investor or Consortium Investors'. Although first published in the 1990s, it still provides timeless advice on what business angels want – and what puts them off. In the latter category, the authors report the following to be regular deal breakers, and my own experience concurs:

O **Poor return on investment:** Angels want a minimum return of 30 per cent or more.

O **Angels want to have fun making money:** A profitable but boring idea might not be enough.

O **Too technical:** The best angels like to invest in what they understand.

O **Excessive valuations:** If angel and entrepreneur can't agree on the worth of the business in five years' time, they won't agree on how much should be invested today.

O **Location:** Angels want an investment they can visit.

O **Product needs 'missionary selling':** Has the customer used this sort of product before? Must they make big changes in order to use it, or will its benefits be instantly familiar?

O **Creature comforts:** Angels typically don't want to pay salaries or pay off existing loans.

O **The entrepreneur themselves:** Angels want to see optimism, determination and drive. The search for funding is tough – it can put out the very spark that angels need to see before they'll invest.

Venture capitalists: on another wavelength

Thanks to the nineties dotcom boom and the business media's love of start-ups, almost everyone now has some idea about venture capital. Sadly, that idea usually tends to be wrong.

Too many entrepreneurs think formal venture capital is the place to look for start-up funding, when in reality venture capitalists tend to focus on making very large bets in industries like high technology and biotech. In short, VC money is probably not for you if you're just starting out. Operations in mainstream sectors like retailing and restaurants almost invariably secure backing not from VCs but from angel investors, high-net-worth individuals or the founder's savings.

Funding start-ups and new technology is exceedingly risky, but it has enabled the development of many of the most important companies of the last fifty years, including DEC, Intel, FedEx, Cisco and Google. Most of them, of course, are US based. That is where most of the world's true venture capital is managed. The failure rate is high, and the expertise needed in spotting and monitoring potential winners is immense. Finding and scrutinizing the right ideas to back is hard work and takes talent and experience. And if such ambitious start-ups are to work, they usually benefit from the technical support and hands-on input from VC investors.

If you're starting small, don't concern yourself with hunting down VC backing.

Banks

How to describe the relationship between banks and the entrepreneur? Robert Frost put it best: 'A bank is a place where they lend you an umbrella in fair weather and ask for it back again when it begins to rain.'

Just as many entrepreneurs are wrong to seek funding from VCs, many less-confident entrepreneurs are wrong to look to their high-street bank for help. While it's true that many successful businesses are built on a bank loan, a high-street bank is still a poor choice of capital for many – and it's because banks are naturally risk averse.

The culture of angels and VCs is that they're in the business of risking money to make money, but banks are in the business of not losing money. Banks like short odds, short timelines, and working with a safety net – such as your house. This brings us to my golden rule: never, ever give to an investor a personal guarantee, and if at all possible, avoid putting the family home on the line.

Any scheme can fail, and to suffer the agony of possible personal bankruptcy as well as seeing your business close is too high a price. So when your investor asks, just say no – and find another bank or backer. They are out there somewhere.

When Howard Schultz was trying to raise $1.25 million in 1985 for the enterprise that would ultimately become Starbucks, he took a year to do it, and presented to 242 possible investors. But in the end he got there – and the lucky early shareholders have seen their investment multiply over a hundred-fold. As Persius said: 'He conquers who endures.'

Secondary sources of money

In the hunt for funding, it's not unusual for entrepreneurs to run out of traditional options before long. It needn't mean that their pitch is flawed.

You're just as likely to be turned down on subjective grounds. For example, some angels only invest in what they know; others like to mix it up. Some VCs think consumer technology is hot; many don't. The bank might have liked your pitch but been prevented from lending simply because of some recent head-office edict. Perhaps people trust your business partner less than they trust you. The list of possible reasons for refusal is truly infinite, and often the real reason is never made clear.

If you're still satisfied that the problem lies with your luck and not your business plan, you should keep plugging away. There's always another source of funding. To name but a few:

O There are myriad grants available from local and central government agencies – even the EU. Grant applications are both a chore and a skill, but for some niches, particularly social or regional businesses, there is a surprising range of options on offer. Many grants seek to do something other than make a quick return, which might lower the bar for you.

O Leasing equipment, rather than buying it, might provide headroom if all else fails, although it tends to be expensive money with rapid repayment schedules.

O Pushing suppliers for extra credit, as a new operator, won't make you popular but old hands will at least understand.

O If you're already trading, consider invoice discounting/factoring – in essence, obtaining money against proof of future revenues, such as a big order. It is always a popular form of funding for companies that have solid debtor/receivable books. Also, lending on stock/inventories from asset-based lenders like GMAC and Burdale may provide a line of finance where conventional banks cannot help.

Remember: outstanding teams with sound propositions will somehow find the money – even if it takes a hell of a lot of shoe leather.

A word about dumb money

Anyone who's ever read a boys' comic will be familiar with the figure of the eccentric millionaire. He's the monocled and top-hatted moneybags who pops up in the final frame to save the day by getting his wallet out.

Obviously real life isn't like that – unless your business is restaurants, wine, art, music or movies, in which case eccentric millionaires crop up amusingly often.

With restaurants, with films, with wine: there seems to be an inexhaustible supply of dumb money that thinks it sounds fun not only to consume the output but invest in it too. There is no end to the lengths some investors will go to in order to acquire a product that will lend them an air of sophistication or high living. Hard-bitten business folk regularly dissolve all good sense by sinking money into a vineyard in Tuscany or a clothing collection touted by the Hollywood actress du jour.

I am sure it is much easier to remain disciplined when considering deploying capital in the chemical industry or in building products. But the romance and the buzz of being involved professionally in the more glamorous sectors seem to overcome all normal objections, and even hard-headed capitalists end up making beginners' errors.

'There was a time
when a fool and
his money were
soon parted, but
now it happens to
everybody'

Adlai Stevenson

Professional investors and angels are usually demanding and exacting types – experience has taught them to be that way. To the struggling entrepreneur, it might sound wonderful to win backing from a smitten millionaire footballer who doesn't ask too many questions – it'd certainly feel like a welcome break from the scrutiny of a hard-nosed angel – but be careful what you wish for.

The best entrepreneurs learn from their investors, so get one you can learn from. A good investor will bring a multi-layered network of contacts and be able to offer advice on strategy, recruitment and potential customers. The budding entrepreneur can acquire a little of the magic simply by listening to their investors' needs and concerns.

No one could blame you for taking money wherever you find it, but try to find smart money first and don't get frustrated when you hear about an actor sinking their money into a hot new restaurant. In my experience, both the actor and restaurateur might soon regret it.

I conclude that if you're starting a simple, service-based business that doesn't require tons of capital, you should moonlight until you've done enough to prove to an angel investor that your fledgling idea has wings.

Part 5
FORMULAS

The trouble with trying to spot a winner

Entrepreneurs are a badly understood breed. If academics, investors, civil servants and politicians were more familiar with the entrepreneur tribe, returns on capital would improve and industrial policy would be more effective.

Yet, after many years of partnering with a variety of business founders, I have some sympathy with anyone researching the psychological make-up of the entrepreneur. Founders are by nature individualistic and hard to analyse. Literature on the subject is neither extensive nor profound; given the importance of entrepreneurs to job and wealth creation, it is a costly omission.

Academics have tried over the decades to categorize entrepreneurs, so as to provide insight into their motivations and likelihood of success. For example, Robert Hornaday proposed a simple division between 'craftsmen', 'promoters' and 'professional managers'. The first type take great pride in the technical aspects of their products; the second are wheeler-dealers who concentrate on making money; the final subspecies have a structured approach to their trade, adopting many of the habits of large corporations. Craftsmen are passionate about quality, but often insufficiently ambitious. Promoters lack a long-term perspective. Professional managers can build scale, but may be too inflexible.

Orvis Collins predated this work, with a study in the early sixties. In *Enterprising Man* (Michigan State University Press, 1964), he and his colleague David Moore wrote about 'trained' entrepreneurs, who study MBAs; 'like father, like son' types, who inherit a family business; and 'opportunistic' entrepreneurs, who seize chances as they arise. And in the work of researcher Douglas Gray we find an extensive set of typologies, including soloists, inventor-researchers, acquirers, speculators, lifestyle entrepreneurs and conglomerators.

In all this work there is a degree of confusion between personality types and outcomes. For example, a 'promoter' might become a 'conglomerator', and a 'professional manager' might be an 'acquirer' or an 'inventor-researcher'. It all seems rather academic, in every sense of the word. What interests me most are psychologies, backgrounds and spotting winners.

Of course, actual people do not fit into theoretical definitions. By their nature, entrepreneurs are rule-breakers who do not conform to sets of rules about their traits and what inspires them. If their magic could be simply identified, it would be a straightforward matter to recognize and back future business champions.

Any venture capitalist will tell you how hard it is to know in advance which business prospects will turn into the big hits, and which will stumble and fail.

I like to think my judgment about prospective business partners is getting better, as it should after decades of trying. But there are no guarantees. The most impressive characters can suffer commercial disasters, and the most robust can have breakdowns. I read endless lists of what to look for and what to guard against. But that sort of perfection is impossible in the real world; we are all flawed and, anyway, many of the true stars would never tick all the boxes.

However, I do hold one firm view about entrepreneurs: strengths are more important than weaknesses. If you have one or two remarkable talents, they may carry you to the top in spite of many shortcomings. So, if you are a wonderful salesman, or a brilliant inventor, or a phenomenal picker of people – it might be enough, even if you are a poor general manager.

Entrepreneurs are not typically well-rounded human beings. Like artists, writers and other creative people, entrepreneurs have a mission and a skill they feel an overwhelming urge to pursue. In addition, drive and energy are necessary attributes, while luck and a special ingredient such as those listed above are also required.

Even with a comprehensive databank that enabled an exhaustive examination of every living entrepreneur, no one could deliver sure-fire predictions. The sheer breadth of personalities who ascend to the summit shows that there is no single gene for success. I think we can all take comfort from that.

Five questions I ask myself before investing

How good is the management team?

o The quality of the management of a business is the acid test. If I do not like the people who run the show, forget it. I do not ignore instinct – if my gut feeling tells me the operators are useless, I walk away. Management must have achieved things in their career. Do not back mad no-hopers who are always punting a crazy new idea. These types will lose you money. Look for winners who are obsessive about their business and who can demonstrate past performance.

o Make sure the management team is honest. Working with crooks as partners is a gruesome experience. I recall putting a small amount of money into a tiny print company. Unfortunately, as soon as I invested the sales collapsed, although the business continued to use a constant amount of paper. The operator was doing business off the books, avoiding the taxman and me. I very quickly sold him my shares at a loss.

o Managers must have high energy levels and be totally motivated. If they are sickly then the enterprise is doomed – no one who is ill can cope with the demands of building a profitable undertaking. Most importantly, the managers must have knowledge and experience of the trade: they must know the technology, the customers, the competitors and the best staff.

O Finally, many of the best management have a large part of their wealth tied up in the enterprise. Most entrepreneurs are at least partly motivated by money, and to have cash at risk helps focus the mind and management's interests with those of shareholders.

Is this company going to win big?

O Rather than dealing in and out of endless marginal situations, I look for investments that have the potential to grow substantially, where I can double, treble or quadruple my money. These are the investments that really make the difference to me.

O Ideally I want to see companies which can expand their sales, margins and their multiple. In other words, I pursue situations which will attract a higher P/E ratio over time, having demonstrated significant organic growth in sales and profits.

O Generally I ignore nice, safe little businesses with limited upside. An investment portfolio will only really perform once it's found a few of the fabled 'ten-baggers' (stocks which rise tenfold). Such investments will allow you to end up with excellent returns despite several miserable performers. Both Peter Lynch and Warren Buffett – two of the legendary investors of our time – agree that longer-term investing in outstanding companies produces above-average returns. The effective private investor focuses on a few sound businesses, running winners and dropping losers.

Have they found a solid niche?

O It's unusual to find big new British companies growing rapidly. I am much more likely to identify opportunities with vast upside among small, specialist companies. Such businesses should possess decent barriers to entry, be it a brand, patent, contracts, franchise or other proprietary situation. Ideally the company should be unique, since it must compete against large competitors who will be better financed. In the real world such companies should have products or services that are evolutionary rather than revolutionary, since markets can take years to accept radical changes. Such drawn-out plays can produce low annualized returns that fail to match those produced by small companies delivering follow-on, adapted technology that is usually quicker to profit.

Is this firm making sales today, or hoping for sales in future?

O I want companies that have sales and can market. I tend to avoid entrepreneurs with marvellous gadgets with no proven commercial potential. The hardest thing in business is to build sales from scratch for a new business – so I prefer to support an entrepreneur who understands the marketplace and how to satisfy it. I avoid research-and-development specialists who do not understand the importance of distribution and coping with the competition.

Do management understand the numbers? Do *I* understand them?

O I read all available information about the prospective project – be it an annual report, a prospectus, business plan, budget or management accounts. You need to clearly explain the key facts about the profitability, balance sheet and cash flow of the company.

O You should identify any obviously scary items, and get me comfortable with them – or give up. There will always be another deal. If the transaction reveals itself as a stinker, I will walk away no matter how much time and effort I have devoted to the proposal.

O I must believe the numbers, and know how the funding and cash cycles and margins will work for the business in question. Only then can I make sensible valuation comparisons with other opportunities and make the right yes/no decision.

Business plans

I spend a lot of my time studying business plans from entrepreneurs who are looking for investment. Many are impressive, but some are ghastly. Among the worst offences:

O **Aggressive confidentiality clauses and an over-obsession about non-disclosure agreements:** I find this sort of pushy legal stuff very off-putting, especially for start-ups. Often you are expected to sign up to very rigid terms without even knowing anything about the proposition. In such circumstances I just turn the deal down flat. If the entrepreneurs distrust me that much they ought to seek backing elsewhere. Would-be restaurateurs are often the worst offenders – would I really bother stealing their idea?

O **Overly technical documents:** Business plans should be written in layman's terms and avoid all jargon and endless acronyms. They should be readable and accessible, not obscure. Inventors can get too wrapped up in their subject – they forget that there are always thousands of projects seeking money. And promoters often use long-winded gobbledegook to disguise a fundamentally bad idea. If I can't understand the deal, then I don't get involved.

O **Lack of focus:** Plans that cover too much territory and companies that try to do too much at once don't appeal to me. Successful concepts are mostly simple, and successful entrepreneurs generally concentrate on a finite market and product range.

O **Preposterous valuations:** Obviously things that are far too expensive go straight in the bin. Such plans usually work back from a daft conclusion based on wild future projections, or spurious comparisons. Instead valuations should be based on sensible estimates of what investors would actually pay. Of course this means you miss the odd Facebook, but I can live with that.

O **Sketchy biographies:** These should be honest and full. They are perhaps the single most important part of the entire proposal. I want to really know the owners and individuals who will make the thing happen. Vague or brief CVs make me suspicious. The chief executive and finance director's résumés are the ones that matter: big-name non-executives cannot compensate for weak executive management who are actually running the business.

O **Weak numbers:** This is really critical. The funding requirement, the estimated returns, and the cash-flow projections – these must be attractive and sufficiently ambitious to be worthwhile. No one is going to put huge effort into a project that will never grow beyond one man and his dog. The figures should all be stated up front in an uncomplicated format. Do not bury them at the back of the pack. Everyone knows whatever you budget will be wrong, but a target to aim for is better than nothing.

The key calculation is your cash break-even point; once you hit this revenue and cost combination, you know you can survive – then you can build.

O **Ignorance of the competition:** All capable entrepreneurs know their competition well. If they say they have none they are fooling themselves. A solid business plan has plenty of specifics about their rivals, and why their particular proposition has a genuine competitive advantage.

O **Perfection:** Every situation is flawed, and if you look for an opportunity with no drawbacks then you will never invest in anything. I quite like deals with a known problem, because then it can be addressed and the price can be adjusted to compensate.

O **Huge appendices and too many spreadsheets:** These might be necessary for loan applications, but equity investors tend to decide based on a few key points. All the supportive evidence and background material can be supplied later if the proposal is of real interest. Don't bury the hooks with padding.

O **Getting someone else to write it:** It shows when advisors rather than principals author a plan – it lacks authenticity. By all means have experts critique your work but actually do the first draft yourself.

O **Too much paper:** Do not rely on the post, or present would-be backers with voluminous amounts of paper. Just get their email address and send them the core presentation online. Catch their attention early and it may lead to something.

O **Unbelievable margins, profits and returns:** Plans that suggest your company will quickly achieve operating margins of 35 per cent, returns on capital of 100 per cent and so on are not credible. Be realistic and conservative and you are more likely to be taken seriously.

Writing a compelling business plan is an art. It should give a venture the best possible chance of securing finance, and it is worth taking huge care over the task.

A list of don'ts

There are quite a few advisors out there helping start-up companies – banks, accountants, small-business agencies. Much of what they say is sensible enough. But few of these mentors have actually done it themselves. So allow me to present to you a handful of things entrepreneurs should *not* do when taking the plunge into self-employment.

O **Do not leave your job.** Moonlight until your idea takes off.

O **Do not rent fancy commercial premises.** Initially use your home or garage. And if you have to get space, make sure it's short term, like serviced offices. Bill Gates started Microsoft in an Albuquerque

motel room. Do not be vain about such matters –
low costs are everything.

○ **Do not be put off by the prospect of a downturn.**
Many great companies are founded when times
are tough, and often remarkable opportunities
arise despite the economy struggling. I took control of PizzaExpress in 1992 – when Britain was in
recession – and it changed my career.

○ **Do not spend money on advertising.** Especially
for fledgling enterprises, PR is a much better bet.
There are so many media outlets now, thanks to the
digital revolution, that any new product or service can get some editorial coverage if you try hard
enough. And not only is PR much cheaper – editorial
attention has much more impact.

○ **Do not engage expensive advisors.** Teach yourself the basics of commercial law, accountancy,
property and so forth. All these professionals will
charge substantial fees to tell you things you can
discover easily online or in beginners' handbooks.
By gaining a solid understanding of these disciplines you will make much better informed decisions. For complex matters, like a 120-page lease,
you will need advice; but simple things like regis-
tering a company you can do yourself.

○ **Do not take on partners in a rush.** By all means
work with others, but tread cautiously before actually setting up in business with someone. You need
to know someone well – their motivation, their ambition, their honesty – before embarking on such

'Do not stop
thinking of life
as an adventure.
You have no
security unless
you can live
bravely, excitingly,
imaginatively;
unless you
can choose a
challenge instead
of a competence'

Eleanor Roosevelt

a journey together. Running a company is often a demanding affair, and incompatibilities soon come out. Work initially on a trial basis as a partnership before making binding commitments.

O **Do not go ahead if your spouse or partner is against it.** Make sure they are totally supportive of your plans. It is almost impossible to succeed in the challenging task of building a new business if you have huge domestic upheaval too. I married fairly late – perhaps partly because I didn't want personal responsibilities to stop me from taking risks.

O **Don't be over-ambitious.** By all means dream of reaching the stars, but start on a realistic scale and grow. Develop a pilot, make it work, prove the concept, and then seize the day. There will always be unexpected problems and obstacles. Learn how to overcome them while operations are small.

O **Don't be lazy or impatient about research and homework.** Know your market intimately. Study your prospective customers and rivals obsessively. Learn everything you possibly can about your scheme: costs, technical issues, staff needs, pricing, marketing and so on. Prepare a comprehensive business plan, even if you don't need finance, simply as a discipline.

A spell in service

I recall giving a speech at an event hosted by Walpole, the association for makers of British luxury goods. In conversation with the senior executives, we all agreed: it is not so much the *products* you sell which guarantees success but the *service* you provide to customers.

I have spent most of my career in the service industries. My big winners have invariably been companies that managed to capture customers with outstanding service, be it retailing, private health-care, recruitment or financial services.

Great service generates repeat custom, loyalty and word-of-mouth recommendation. Nothing is better at creating a powerful franchise. Yet it is extraordinary how bad service can be in the hospitality industry in Britain – even at expensive hotels and restaurants. That is why there remain wonderful opportunities in the sector: so many of the opposition are still doing the job so badly.

After all, what do people want when they go for a meal or a room for the night? A warm welcome, prompt attention and knowledgeable staff. They want personal recognition if they are a regular. They want consistency, courtesy and efficiency. And they want any problems dealt with swiftly and politely.

My experience, from owning classic restaurants like Le Caprice, The Ivy and J Sheekey, is that diners might consider food, wine, value and décor important, but what really matters to them is how they are treated

'Businesses planned for service are apt to succeed; businesses planned for profit are apt to fail'

Nicholas Butler

as people. When eating out, the public complain about noise, prices, bad food, crowds, cleanliness and so forth; but over two-thirds of all complaints relate to poor service.

At PizzaExpress, I made sure I saw every single customer-complaint letter.

Frequently the issue was about how managers dealt with difficulties. The best managers know that you can turn around the most dissatisfied customer by exceeding their expectations. So if their meal has been slow, give them a drink – or possibly the entire meal – on the house. You may well switch them from being harsh critics to advocates: a complaint that's well handled often leads to repeat business.

In theory, delivering memorable service should not be difficult: the principles are straightforward. But the task of persuading employees to deliver excellent service on every occasion is hard.

The first step is to hire nice people, who are responsive and like dealing with the public.

Cultivate a sense of pride in the organization.

Instil the belief from the top to the bottom that the customer comes first.

Pay staff well, and reward them extra for above-average performance.

Provide strong leadership, show them respect, and give them the correct equipment and support.

Training can help – but I think picking the right individuals who enjoy their work is more important.

Culture matters enormously. While French waiters are usually highly professional, they are also too often haughty – sometimes almost rude. I find this sort of clipped manner, all too evident in certain grand boutiques in London, to be off-putting. On the other hand, Americans tend to understand real service. I buy my shirts at Brooks Brothers in New York because the store assistants take immense care of me. They are hired and incentivized properly. But when I've been to their shops in London the experience has been hugely disappointing. Similarly I think the Four Seasons hotel chain in the US tends to give remarkable levels of service. Overall service standards tend to be much lower in the UK.

The fascinating thing is that good service does not necessarily cost a firm more to deliver than shoddy service. It is an obvious way for entrepreneurs to gain an edge and take share from rivals without requiring additional investment.

But it does need constant effort and a skilled team. Moreover, customers are becoming more assertive in showing their dissatisfaction. Thanks to websites like Tripadvisor.com and Qype.com, bad experiences are communicated for the world to see.

The hit-and-run approach to customers is not a sustainable business model. Be it tourism, sales, administration or after-care, every business should excel at service if it wants to prosper.

Some businesses manage to give bad service and still prosper, for a while – but would you want your name above the door?

'To give real
service you must
add something
which cannot
be bought or
measured with
money, and that
is sincerity and
integrity'

Donald Adams

By the staff, for the staff

Every business gets it wrong sometimes. I recall sitting, increasingly miserable, in an establishment I owned at the time, watching as a catalogue of incompetence saw a series of customers treated poorly. I couldn't bear it for very long before I intervened. Without customers, there is nothing. On this occasion, the staff were too busy dealing with 'internal' matters to attend to the very people who justify the whole undertaking.

Coincidentally, on the same day, I was treated to a classic piece of poor service and inflexibility by British Airways. It made me wonder if it will survive in any recognizable form.

I fear that, as so often happens, BA has become an institution run not for the benefit of its customers but for its staff and pensioners. Its shareholders, meanwhile, have long been forgotten. It suffers from all the weaknesses of an ex-monopoly now facing ferocious competition and a terrible economy. BA cabin crew typically earn much more than staff at rival airlines – and BA has a huge pension burden that its competitors do not.

BA has a high-cost model, and has come to depend on juicy-margin passengers in first and business class. That income stream is heavily dependent on the business cycle to an extent that lower-cost airlines are not. BA still charges significantly more than no-frills operators, and justifies this by calling itself a 'full-service' airline even though my experience is that its service levels are no better than those of low-cost operators.

In any climate, customers seek value for money regardless of the ticket price – and customers will desert an expensive offering for a cheaper one if the quality is indistinguishable. Management at BA are perpetually engaged in a war on costs, understandably, but the union's answer to this massive challenge smacks of industrial suicide: they routinely threaten to go on strike, further alienating the customer.

BA shows how easy it is for an organization to become hijacked by its staff, and turn inwards as a result.

The Royal Mail is another example. It is an ex-monopoly now facing competition on many fronts. Technology is destroying the traditional letter as a means of communication at alarming speed. When everyone has a broadband connection, the need for traditional postal provision may well disappear altogether. Our postmen appear to do a conscientious job but the organization urgently needs to modernize and scrap archaic working practices.

Efficient newcomers and online alternatives mean the Royal Mail has a huge battle on its hands. Its staff are paid more than the private sector, their productivity is low and the organization has a colossal pension deficit.

The Royal Mail has the luxury of being government owned, and its union contributes to the Labour Party's coffers, which give it some protection when that party is in power. But the grim reality of the market will intervene sooner or later. Again, the union response to reform is to strike. Each time this happens, customers switch, never to return – steadily bleeding the organization to death.

Even vast companies with seemingly impregnable market positions can fail if they lose sight of why they are in business.

General Motors had the supreme arrogance of a company with 40 per cent of all US car sales. But it pandered to its employees and the unions, failed to understand its customers and eventually needed a $50-billion government rescue. The demoralized and shrunken entity is now emerging from bankruptcy, having sunk to as little as 10 per cent of the US market at one low point.

The emerging entrepreneur might look at these struggling behemoths and wonder where the lesson might be: is every enterprise condemned to ossify once it employs more than a certain number of workers?

I think not. Consider the John Lewis Partnership, the British department store and grocery chain. Here the staff really do own the business, and behave like enlightened capitalists and not bloody-minded union members. It delivers world-class service mainly because its ownership model generates staff that consider their interest and the customer's interest to be one and the same thing.

Independents will always have their day

I once came across a brilliant toyshop in Boston with a notice in its window about the importance of indie businesses. It argued that there is a passion and engagement within an independent enterprise that large corporates can only envy.

As a customer, I have a huge amount of empathy with that view. The nascent entrepreneur, operating in the face of powerful and corporate competitors, can take courage from it.

I like the individuality of an owner-managed organization. I want a merchant I patronize to have character, not to be a faceless entity. I see many of the founders of these types of companies as artisan entrepreneurs, who are willing to apply superhuman efforts to make their creations succeed, to make the sort of product that connoisseurs would wish for.

Consequently I prefer staying at boutique hotels to bland chains, and using a family-owned printer when I can. I prefer an idiosyncratic baker or delicatessen to the suffocating uniformity of a big supermarket. In owner-managed businesses, the tone of the experience is more likely to be set by one person's vision, rather than the morass of management layers and product committees which tend to suck the life out of big-company offerings.

Unfortunately, lenders, landlords, suppliers and many other critical partners are biased towards large businesses, which are seen as more reliable and creditworthy. This is to ignore the business advantages enjoyed by small companies, such as low central costs and flexibility normally absent from much larger concerns. Smaller firms may lack buying power and a well-known brand, but they will not have burdens like public shareholders or a pension-fund deficit.

Occasionally a bank manager or vendor will see potential in an emerging business, and go the extra mile to help. They do this because it is more exciting to support an up-and-comer than an established business: everyone would love to be able to say, 'I backed Microsoft when they had five staff.' Absolute engagement of a founder with a lender can sometimes make a difference – corporate executives rarely match that level of involvement and dedication.

Many smaller undertakings are not run primarily for profit. They reflect the personality and ego of their owners, and in some respects are almost closer to social enterprises than classic commerce. This gives them latitude. Family businesses are often run with paternalistic, very long-term objectives in mind. It is hard not to admire that sort of attitude, and see it as a healthy balance to the near-hysteria of quarterly reporting and volatile publicly traded stock prices.

New ideas tend to flourish best in freewheeling environments, not in a bureaucracy – defined by Balzac as a 'giant mechanism operated by pygmies'. Books about boosting innovation and creativity in large corporations rarely sell well – because nobody needs to buy them. It's very rare that any one employee in a megacorp can make much of a difference to the product, so why buy a book about it?

Complications and conflicts arise as you expand a company from small beginnings to something much larger and more profitable. Initially it is a quirky, intimate and highly adaptable organism. But as it expands, there is an inevitable tendency for the journey to become more cautious and boring.

Motivation is gradually diluted as managerialism takes over from seat-of-the-pants risk-taking. Progress is about replication rather than adventure. Early on, money tends to be relevant only as a means of starting the project, rather than as an end in itself. But when banks and outside shareholders get involved, the pressures to perform mount – so the distinctive features fade, to be replaced by the treadmill of financial returns. This is an almost inevitable sequence.

There is no easy answer to this conundrum. Some choose to stay small and perfectly formed. Others are more ambitious, and realize that to compete and satisfy the desires of their staff they need to grow. There is no right rate of growth; typically, entrepreneurs try to expand as fast as the organization possibly can – and then more.

Yet the future might just belong to agile indies and freelancers, not giant corporations.

Massive, cumbersome outfits such as Citigroup in the USA and RBS in the UK have proved that, in spite of their enormous resources and economies of scale, large firms can go monstrously wrong. Many industrial activities can only be carried out by huge concerns with substantial capital – steel production, automotive manufacture, utilities and so forth. Yet few of us have much affection for these dull empires. Their culture must be conformity rather than disruption.

The division between indies and big business isn't a matter of corporate responsibility or ethics. It is more about variety and enlightenment.

Of course, I believe in free-market capitalism and ambition – but I also enjoy the spirit, invention and guts that indies bring to any field. They punch above their weight in terms of innovation and customer service, and force big players to up their game.

In these uncertain times, there is every reason to believe – in spite of the relentless march of globalization – that the indies of the world will continue to thrive. A fledgling entrepreneur should not shy away from injecting their personal foibles into the character of their business – no one really wants to buy from a characterless enterprise, much less work at one.

Franchises – the worst of all worlds

Every so often an overseas restaurant operation contacts me, enquiring if I want to license their business for the British market. I always turn them down, after carefully studying their operation to learn what I can. I have realized that very little can be copyrighted in the food sector. Design, menus, themes: they can all be easily and legally copied. If I were inclined to start a new restaurant chain I would do it myself. I can invent my own brand and recipes; why pay someone who actually needs my expertise in property and people more than I need their brand licence?

But if one considers sectors where there is technology and patent protection, then clearly taking a licence has advantages. Importing an invention, or gaining the rights to make it, might well save huge expenditure on research and development. It is always better to own the intellectual property, but if that is too expensive, too uncertain or will take too long, then being the distributor may make better economic sense. If you are licensing a global name – major celebrities and well-known cartoon characters are often surprisingly happy to oblige – then OK. A joint venture is an even better solution: that way the rights holder has an even greater vested interest in ensuring the project succeeds.

There are those who would have you believe that a franchise is the best of all worlds, offering the strength of a brand coupled with the freedom of being your own boss. The franchise industry certainly has its visible successes – nearly every Subway, McDonald's, 7–Eleven and Dunkin' Donuts is a franchise, with the branding being rented by individual private owners. But consider the atmosphere in those establishments. Do they have the buzz of an owner-managed business, or do the staff generally look and sound like tiny cogs in a giant machine?

Too often, a franchise combines the claustrophobia of corporate life with all the risks of running your own show.

Some years ago I sat on the board of the British Franchise Association, and became slightly cynical about the industry. For start-ups there can be some

logic in paying fees for an established brand with genuine customer goodwill, and a business format that
cannot easily be replicated. But in a lot of cases the
franchisee ends up making a meagre living, while the
franchisor collects handsome royalties and has no
capital invested or at risk.

Generally I would advise new entrepreneurs to
avoid signing up to a franchise unless they feel it is a
special one. Unfortunately too many of the formats
widely available are low quality, and a few are nothing more than a rip-off. There are countless magazines,
trade shows and websites given over to the selling of
franchises – perhaps a warning in itself. Too many franchises exist only to be sold, not to be bought and run.

Above all, if you rent someone else's idea, with all
the restrictions that entails, then you do not control
your own destiny – which is part of the satisfaction of
being your own boss.

Pride of ownership is an important motivator for
most entrepreneurs: and that element is diminished if
you are a member of a franchise system. You may find
that growth is restricted, and you will almost certainly receive a reduced sum for your business when you
come to sell.

Be highly suspicious if you are offered a relatively
obscure, second-hand franchise for sale. The vendor
has probably discovered that the system doesn't work,
and you are likely to have the same difficulties if you
proceed.

Better to start with a clean sheet, and either put
your own name above the door or buy someone else's
good name outright.

Part 6
THE CYCLE

Turnaround and creative destruction

All businesses and industries are cyclical, and that boom and bust comes to virtually every company. It is human nature to become exuberant at the top and depressed at the bottom – such a roller coaster is the essence of life. I would go so far as to say in general I prefer the company of those who have highs and lows, rather than someone whose mood is flat and unchanging. Those dull spirits remind me of entropy, and all life is engaged in a perpetual battle to resist that.

I recall giving a speech at the annual conference for the Institute for Turnaround, a trade body for company doctors, those mostly low-profile figures who try to salvage insolvent companies. I liken them to corporate firemen: they walk into burning companies, seeing whether they can find anything to retrieve from the flames and ashes. These unsentimental, almost heroic figures become frenetically busy when the economy turns down. Their job is to revive what should be saved, and close the rest. Their tales of business comebacks can be both inspiring and scary.

My favourite comeback tale of modern times is the remarkable achievements of Carlos Ghosn, CEO and president at Renault and Nissan Motor Company. He arrived in 1999, when the business lost $2.7 billion and had $22 billion of debt. Within five years he had grown profits to $5 billion and the firm was almost debt free. He carried out this astounding rehabilitation by shaking up the way Japanese corporations did things, combined with plenty of hard work and common sense. All very straightforward stuff, but never easy to do.

When the economy collapses inevitably there are many organizations that collapse with it. Some die quickly, others may require the equivalent of open-heart surgery – a massive procedure that may kill or cure. For a portion of these, the experience will unleash new vigour, new ambitions and new talents.

When times are good and money is easy, we all misallocate capital. This leads to waste and an eventual reckoning. As the wheel inevitably turns and conditions deteriorate, so credit tightens, companies fail and assets are recycled. This is an irresistible sequence of events. Mere mortals cannot resist the tide of history. Markets and exchanges are merely mechanisms that reflect the temperament of man.

Witnessing and participating in such upheaval can be traumatic. Take the collapse of Lehman Brothers and the forced sell-offs of Merrill Lynch and HBoS. For the staff, their families, and other stakeholders, this classic example of Schumpeter's 'creative destruction' is hardly something to be celebrated. Here is a sudden and jolting reallocation of resources. Overnight, venerable institutions are destroyed, and new ones spring up, phoenix-like, to fill the gap. But this process of renewal is at the heart of capitalism. Inefficient and misguided organizations disappear and ultimately more productive ones arise.

Nothing is permanent and all organizations must reinvent themselves periodically – or die. The market is a great leveller. Even the mighty are humbled, or as the Tiger Lillies' song 'The Crack of Doom' has it: '. . . every empire turns to dust'.

Of course value is also destroyed in this violent process of reordering – but without such a threat, which institution would ever undertake the painful restructuring that is a part of staying relevant and competitive?

So many industries I know – media, retailing, financial services, leisure – have to adapt to a rapidly evolving market. Banks are learning that financial engineering tricks are not enough. Shopkeepers, publishers and broadcasters realize that the online threat is very real indeed.

There is a palpable sense of urgency which would be absent if the pressure were not real. The relentless march of technology and globalization is forcing the pace. This is how things get done; this is how institutions and societies progress and improve.

The cycle is endless, and so budding entrepreneurs would do well to familiarize themselves with the characteristics of each stage. Few industries follow the cycle quite so faithfully as the restaurant industry.

The cycle as told by restaurants

There has been a steady rise in supply among casual dining chains since I first got involved with PizzaExpress. From gastro-pubs to 'fast casual' operations, the restaurant industry has mushroomed. Meanwhile costs have risen materially: rents and business rates, utility bills, wages and food costs have all climbed.

Returns are lower than they used to be, and are unlikely to recover to the halcyon days of the 1990s. Then even a relative amateur like me could grow a business enjoying 20 per cent unit margins and cash returns well over 35 per cent. Competition was limited, sites were fairly plentiful, rents were bearable and demand was rising.

But, as the cycle would have it, bumper profits attracted more and more capital and so more capacity appeared. Excess capacity is a mixed blessing in a boom but lethal in a slump. During a downturn the public mood changes, so that restaurant meals become discretionary spending while items like mortgage payments do not. All those empty seats in restaurants become a burden when the lights have to be kept on regardless.

Of course, as restaurant guru Tim Zagat once said in the *New York Times*, 'People still have to eat.' Every restaurateur hopes the eating out habit has become so entrenched that customers are extremely loath to give it up. Certainly fast-food and mid-market restaurants are likely to weather any storm better than big-ticket retailers like furniture shops, car dealers, travel agents or electronics stores. And of course the restaurant business doesn't face the Internet threat battering mainstream shops: you can't exactly eat out online.

Moreover, there is a belief that in stressful times the public want distraction and entertainment, and perhaps a glass to calm anxieties. A meal out can offer a few hours of fun, away from worries about job security and the economy. And for those working harder than ever to make ends meet, they just won't have the time to shop and cook at home.

Of course, high-end establishments are vulnerable to a clampdown on expense-account meals. Those places that rely on extravagant business functions always struggle in downturns. Every business I've ever known cuts back such spending when times are tough – partly to save cash, and partly as a gesture towards the new climate of austerity. Meanwhile individuals shop around and look for value offerings. Many restaurants maintain sales by discounting, sacrificing margin to preserve volumes.

The cycle also exposes the folly of loading up with too much debt. When times are good, the larger restaurant chains undergo leveraged buyouts at ever-higher multiples – in other words, they borrow more money relative to their revenue and profits, or are bought by private equity operators who borrow the purchase price. Many chains are left with a legacy of debt from the mergers-and-acquisitions merry-go-round.

'… the internet won't change the way we chew gum'

Warren Buffett, buying shares in Wrigley's at the height of the dotcom boom

If profits deteriorate then those operators may breach promises made to the banks, with control of the business passing back to the banks. For certain owners, the threat of such action prompts cutbacks on staff, refurbishment and other capital expenditure, and perhaps even the quality of ingredients. This always seems easier than improving the offering, in the short term at least, and it's certainly easier than raising prices at a time when consumers knowingly have less money to spend.

It might seem that a downswing in the cycle is hardly good news for participants like me – but only on the face of it. Recessions offer opportunities to make distress purchases of sound businesses from operators who've run into trouble. A rising tide of success over recent decades has transformed confidence in the restaurant as an asset class.

Perhaps the best thing one can say about tough times is that they always separate those who have been lucky from those who truly know what they are doing. Management who run a tight ship and have a solid-value, differentiated concept can take share from over-borrowed, over-priced players with a bland proposition.

As always, the strong get stronger and the weak fall by the wayside, though no one stays on top for ever. That is the cycle at work, and it never stops.

Managing in a downturn

In good times, board meetings concern themselves with exciting things such as capital expenditure plans, acquisitions, senior appointments, new projects and budgets for growth. Inevitably, the items on the agenda are rather more sombre in a downturn. Redundancies feature often.

Short of shutting the company, there is nothing more demoralizing for most entrepreneurs than having to sack people. Usually it is a case of sacrificing the few to save the many. At this stage, a lot of the departures are voluntary – employees taking pay-offs to retire early and so forth. But the legislated consultation process means the affair is painfully drawn out, a classic case of state interference leading to increased unhappiness on all sides.

In bad times, another major discussion point every month is debtors (also known as payables). Are debtor days (the amount of time it takes customers to actually pay you) increasing and have there been many bad debts? Where has credit insurance cover been pulled? Which customers could go bust? If a customer does go bust, do we still legally own the goods we've supplied, or have we lost our stock for ever?

There is pressure to generate cash, because the bank facilities of yesteryear are just a memory. A bank that was formerly happy to let a company trade on overdraft might suddenly insist that it stays in the black every month, which for many is impossible. Instead of waiting for the post, suppliers send a courier to wait

'When the profits of trade happen to be greater than ordinary, over-trading becomes a general error both among great and small dealers'

Adam Smith

in reception to collect a cheque. After all, you cannot meet a payroll on excuses.

Meanwhile, corporations go through agonies in getting their year-end audit signed off. Even giant companies can struggle with the key 'going-concern statements' in their accounts – basically a promise to shareholders that, all things considered, the company can continue to trade for the next twelve months. An audit partner once told me of a massive, hugely profitable company with more than £10 billion of debt that needed to be authorized by the bank for a further year – and at that stage the bank wasn't promising anything. When it comes to problems arising from follies of spending, big businesses are ultimately no different from the rest of us.

In these circumstances, audit committee meetings are prolonged and tense because the auditors do not want to be sued if things go horribly wrong in six months, and no one wants to be prosecuted for misleading shareholders.

And, for the indebted, there are bank covenants – promises made to the bank in return for obtaining a loan. Covenants keep finance directors up at night. My contacts at the major lenders tell me many hundreds of corporate borrowers breached covenants in the credit crunch, especially in sectors such as retailing, construction and capital goods. But the banks cannot call in all their debts and appoint administrators – the wave of insolvencies would drown them. Instead, banks raise rates and charge big fees.

It becomes apparent that many leaders are really just suited to the good times. Some managers have to

'This is no time for ease and comfort. It is the time to dare and endure'

Winston Churchill

be fired because they simply cannot cope. During a severe recession, when growth is irrelevant and all that matters is survival, their bullish attitude and denial of reality becomes positively dangerous. But who of quality is willing to join an ailing concern? There are lots of characters looking for work, but do they have the stamina and resolution for the task?

These are the days when one feels almost physically battered by bad news and there appears to be no light at the end of the tunnel. But then something happens. I recall being in one particular trough of gloom that ended when a reader of my *FT* column reminded me of the extraordinary achievements of Germany and Japan, bankrupt nations virtually reduced to rubble by defeat in the Second World War. Within two decades they had become industrial powerhouses and remain two of the pre-eminent economies in the world. Those countries' enterprise, ingenuity, hard work and discipline delivered them prosperity from the wreckage of absolute defeat.

There is nothing individuals cannot achieve with the right leadership, incentives and culture. Businesses and entire nations can face down difficulties if there is willingness to accept the seriousness of the threats and to reform in the face of them.

Faustian pact of a guarantee

I play tennis at a club in London. One week I noticed in the court next to me a man whose business had collapsed a few weeks previously, after it had borrowed billions of pounds. He was laughing and seemed relaxed. Somehow I doubt he had given any personal guarantees to the banks.

Following his example, whenever I give advice to would-be entrepreneurs I remind them of my golden rule: never, ever give any lender a personal guarantee, and do not put your house on the line. There is always another way to find the money.

I make this point often, and with good reason, but there are always a few borrowers who ignore the advice, and typically one is made aware of them in a recession. A friend who works in property tells me the Irish banks were unable to extract personal guarantees from British developers in the downturn of the late 2000s; it seems their property clients were scarred so badly after the bust in the early 1990s that they learned not to risk all their assets by signing a bit of paper. But in Ireland there were many super-bullish, newly rich house builders and wheeler-dealers who were happy to provide a personal guarantee. Some had never known a crash, and didn't see theirs coming. They were soon descended upon by the banks, like Satan coming to claim Faust's soul.

For someone who is on the hook, that single

commitment of a personal guarantee changes everything.

The gruesome mathematics of leverage in reverse, combined with personally guaranteed debt, means there are always a few minus millionaires around town – tycoons with seven-figure lifestyles and eight-figure debts. In rising markets, building an empire often entails the use of as much debt as possible. And with boom-time banks willing to lend property developers huge sums while requiring relatively little in the way of security, a brave developer can buy entire buildings by putting up as little as a fifth of the purchase price.

But if the property has fallen by a third or more, our developer hasn't just lost his equity; he'll have lost another 15 per cent of the total price – which he now owes the bank. I've heard of players going from a net worth of £500 million to less than nothing in two years.

These situations are characteristic of the property market, where debt is so integral and where the participants can't resist rolling the dice every time. In most cases, as a senior restructuring expert told me, the banks simply put sticking plasters over the problems. Often, syndicates cannot agree on the solution, so a proper fix is simply deferred.

But in other fields, such as digital media, the behaviour and mood are different. Online entrepreneurs fund deals with venture capital or the more sophisticated end of angel capital, where there is rarely recourse to their home if things go wrong. I meet these types, and they seem happier.

I enjoy attending the Founders Forum, an annual conference for entrepreneurs that always features European technology pioneers who have sold their companies for tens or even hundreds of millions. Almost all are under forty-five and are working on their second, third or even fourth Internet start-up. Each time they risk some cash, but obviously keep most of their gains socked away in a bank somewhere. Debt is never an issue because senior lenders refuse to get involved where there is no tangible security or even revenues to service the interest.

That's why venture capitalists are rarely a good source of funding for the average small business start-up: the average VC is interested in backing the next Google. No one in the venture capital world is being threatened by the bailiffs, despite generating more than its fair share of failures. And meanwhile, the online world is still stealing customers, advertising and market share from traditional retailers, publishers and others. So there remains plenty of confidence and a fair amount of capital ready to seize the opportunities.

I spend much of my time dealing with hard choices in stagnant sectors, so it is always refreshing to hear the optimism still apparent in the web world. Long may it continue – and long may investors avoid giving personal guarantees.

A sense of dread ails the opinion-makers

When I give speeches to groups of entrepreneurs, I am invariably asked why the media is so gloomy. I usually reply that journalists believe bad news sells. But I think there is an added, more desperate and personal element to the pessimism: journalists are petrified that their very livelihoods are under threat.

I recall attending a celebratory dinner for hacks at my old Oxford college, Magdalen. Seventy or so writers turned up – foreign correspondents, editors, documentary makers, freelancers. The mood should have been upbeat, but the speeches were doom-laden. Most of the guests I spoke to were worried for their careers and the very future of their profession. They see the local newspaper industry in meltdown, leading dailies and magazines shutting across the US, radio and television broadcasters struggling, and cuts everywhere. The economic downturn has hammered advertising like never before.

The real killer is the Internet: Wikipedia, blogs, Google and all the other free websites are smashing the economics of traditional media organizations. Major outlets have to support loss-making or break-even online operations that are eviscerating their print or broadcast core. Few of the pure new-media players fund any content creation. Revenues, profits, margins and cash flow have collapsed incredibly quickly for almost all established publishers and broadcasters. Their business models are broken.

No wonder journalists are miserable. No one should be surprised that most articles and reports on the economy have a bearish and depressing slant. The authors are probably expecting the sack – or at least a pay cut and a heavier workload. I am reminded in a terrifying way of the 1980s, when I worked alongside typesetters for an advertising agency. These highly skilled craftsmen handled the pre-press element of a print advert. That line of work has disappeared and now so have they, blown away by the relentless advance of technology.

In every downturn, the same dark mood can be felt in banks and financial organizations. Many are full of executives waiting to be fired. Calls are answered by an unfamiliar voice, which sheepishly informs the caller that their old contact no longer works there. Bonuses and expansion plans become history.

No wonder they don't do much lending in a downturn: they're understaffed and depressed. This pervasive sense of dread spreads to analysts, economists and other commentators employed in the City of London and on Wall Street, who offer opinions on the future of markets and business. And, of course, their views are going to be bleak, since they are worried about being laid off, meeting their bills and wondering what they are going to do with themselves now the music has stopped.

Every downturn exposes those industries whose scale and profitability are unsustainable – media and banking being textbook examples. In recent years the US financial sector generated more than 40 per cent of all domestic corporate profits. Historically, newspapers and broadcasters could make operating margins of more than 20 per cent, most of which was free cash flow.

Most of the juicy opportunities from all this disruption are being seized by upstart companies like Facebook, Groupon and others. These times offer once-in-a-lifetime occasions when new companies, unfettered by the baggage of the past, can reinvent whole industries, as the online players are in media. Young firms can evolve and be swift, where giants lumber and stumble.

There are no simple or swift cures for the pain that comes with structural change. Many hundreds of thousands who lose their jobs must reinvent their lives and find new vocations.

After the crash in 1987, various financiers I knew became farmers, painters, shopkeepers, novelists and philanthropists among other occupations. I suspect few ever regretted the move. It can broaden horizons and lead to a healthy realignment of priorities.

All this dislocation is hard to take, but there is little choice. The task is made easier for those who believe there will always be new opportunities, whatever the temporary difficulties.

The consumer's new mantra is value

The most dramatic shift in consumer behaviour one witnesses in a cycle is the trading down from aspirational goods to 'value goods'. It is a sudden, mass migration. In their work and personal lives, consumers cut back and look for a bargain. As always, the best businesses adapt to the new psychology and the rest asphyxiate.

In the good times, nearly every company likes to think of its products as 'aspirational'. It's true there always will be customers willing to pay extra for premium goods, obsessively seeking quality over price. But every such era will wax and wane, and must inevitably give way to the mantra of 'value' – and it doesn't matter which market you're in.

This pronounced trend doesn't happen just because the world is tightening its belt; ostentatious luxury is soon viewed as a social faux pas. That's why at dinner parties, it becomes fine to serve cava where once only champagne would do. Apart from anything, we've always known the two drinks taste the same – it's simply snobbery and clever marketing by the French that has persuaded us to pay four times the price for near identical products.

And as the cycle turns for champagne, so it turns for whole swathes of industries: more-affordable items are purchased at the expense of top-end luxuries.

It always takes a while for the pain to be felt in the

luxury goods business. Initially, all those selling yachts or sports cars or operating casinos think that the dependable rich Russians and Arabs will bail them out, and for a while that's true. But then the price of oil usually collapses in a downturn, just like everything else, and so plutocrats from resource-rich countries must rein in their spending too. Meanwhile, businesses everywhere savagely reduce expense accounts and corporate hospitality, hitting all sorts of suppliers reliant on that spending.

Businesses in the mid-market can prosper in a downturn, but must discount to survive. At the Giraffe restaurant chain, which I chair, we engineer our costs to cope with lower price points and preserve margin. Operators such as Tesco and Wal-Mart push their discount own-label brands and let their suppliers take the hit.

In some cases, it's not about retaining profitability – it's about staying solvent. Industries such as the steel and automotive trades slash their prices and costs, reducing capacity and laying off workers. Only those with strong balance sheets cope with extended periods of trading declines.

Some companies rebase their costs by going through bankruptcy and emerging in a super-competitive condition, having used bankruptcy legislation to shed liabilities such as debt, leases, contracts, pension obligations and so forth. This makes life hard for their better-funded rivals, and can almost have the effect of rewarding bad behaviour. But better the assets are recycled than that whole operations are permanently shut down, with all the jobs simply gone.

More and more services move to no-frills, as consumers shop around via the Internet and focus exclusively on price and the basics. Unless you are the dominant low-cost operator, this can mean a profitless existence for many other organizations, which can keep in line with competitors but regress overall.

The death of demand results in structural overcapacity in many spheres. It can provide a useful trigger to push through necessary streamlining, but in plenty of cases 'cheaper' can mean worse service, fewer features and so on.

Organic, green, fair-trade and other such attributes all make items more expensive. It's much easier to take the moral high ground when you're not worried about losing your job, home or business.

Not all pleasure is eliminated. What I call 'affordable indulgence' usually holds up. Cinema admissions stay strong, because it is a relatively cheap night out that lets us forget the gloom. At Patisserie Valerie our cakes provide a spell of sumptuousness, and sell well throughout downturns. And television viewing generally stays up, in spite of the relentless growth of broadband – because it is 'free'.

All this austerity must eventually give way to a fresh age of excess, though it is always impossible to spot the turning point. You'll only know it's over for sure when it's well and truly over – and by then the true risk-taking entrepreneurs will have already made their moves to bring luxury back to the fore.

'Even these hardships will be grand things to look back on'

Virgil

X & Y in a downturn

They say the X & Y generations are the most entrepreneurial in history. But none of them have been in business during a recession.

This is the service economy era. Younger entrepreneurs I meet are running marketing agencies, web-design firms, recruitment companies, finance businesses, software houses, telecom firms. These operations required limited capital to get going and faced few barriers to entry, compared to periods when heavy industry ruled.

The Internet has helped unleash ambition and enterprise in an unprecedented way. But I worry that a lot of these companies are fragile constructs, not built to weather severe conditions.

For founders who have only ever known expansion, challenging times are a harsh wake-up call. They will suffer bad debts when customers go bust. They experience real cost inflation for the first time in decades – and desperately try to pass on price rises, just when customers are harder to come by. Meanwhile the banks go into meltdown.

These entrepreneurs have never before spent sleepless nights awaiting the phone call from the bank to say that the loan is being called in. You age fast in such adverse circumstances. I can recall fending off a bailiff who brandished something called a walking possession order; he wanted to seize the very desk I was working on.

No one can say in advance who has the constitution

to survive the drawn-out agony of a serious slump. It takes resilience – and cash – to withstand two or three years of grim trading. Maintaining morale while carrying out redundancies and wholesale restructuring can defeat even the finest manager.

But of course things could always be worse. A close friend ran a biomedical business in Beirut during the Lebanese civil war in the 1980s. The currency collapsed, interest rates went to 17 per cent, and staff had to sleep on the plant floor for fear of getting shot by snipers while commuting to work. But somehow they coped. It rather makes everyday trading problems seem trivial.

Unfortunately the burden of government regulation – from employment legislation to health-and-safety rules – means business is less flexible than during previous declines. And low-cost foreign rivals are much more of a threat. Some companies have little fat to cut and are fairly highly operationally geared – many of these will tumble straight into loss if their top-line sales drop by just 20 per cent. Established corporations will have years of retained profits to fall back on – but smaller, newer firms will not.

On the plus side, levels of debt at entrepreneurial companies tend to be lower. In the largest of buyouts, the average debt/equity ratio can be 4 to 1, with interest barely covered by cash flow. These are the highly leveraged deals that go to the wall in tough times.

By contrast, entrepreneurial firms should be more adaptable – and they have the passion and grit of an owner to keep them alive. As they say, progress is an uphill fight to the end.

'An inconvenience
is only an adventure
wrongly considered;
an adventure is only
an inconvenience
rightly considered'

G. K. Chesterton

Dishonest dealings

Early in every commercial career there is a moment of clarity as you learn about underhand behaviour in the business world. It is the realization that, when it comes to money, even seemingly charming fellows are capable of telling serious lies. And deceit comes to the fore in a downturn.

I lost my naivety at the age of twenty-eight, with the company I mentioned in chapter 1's litany of failures. I took assurances from an audit partner that the accounts were accurate and prudent. I didn't realize that the auditor was about to retire, and that he was far too close to the chief executive – so had little to lose by misleading me. In fact the numbers were a fiction; the company almost went bust and I lost lots of money. I became much more sceptical from then on about who and what I believed.

I fear many of the best and most experienced investors acquire a profoundly cynical view of human nature. They have been ripped off too often. I know one fund manager whose faith in his fellow man was obliterated by the bursting of the dotcom bubble. Umpteen directors he thought were his friends had lied to him on the way up. They were nowhere to be found when it all went wrong. He had a breakdown and has given up the profession.

The downturn is the point in the cycle when the truth becomes rather more expendable. Be it in board meetings, annual shareholder meetings, job interviews, contract negotiations, employment tribunals – you

'A lie is an abomination unto the Lord, and a very present help in times of trouble'

Adlai Stevenson

name it, the old *actualité* will buckle under the pressure. Desperation compromises the ethics. Highfalutin talk of moral principles from media pundits and management academics means rather less if your company faces bankruptcy or you face the sack.

During the sub-prime mortgage crisis, we sat transfixed by the unravelling of American capitalism and watched the clamour to find the guilty parties. Most commentators blamed Wall Street. Yet the heart of the wealth destruction was a collapsing sub-prime property market. And in that dark and catastrophic place, I suspect there have been more lies told than by all the world's bankers put together.

It is inconceivable that the many thousands of realtors, mortgage brokers, valuers, developers, builders and other members of the great daisy chain were not in on the game. Moreover, the homeowners themselves were also willing participants. Many lied to get mortgages and bought more houses than they could afford, perhaps thinking they would flip the place for a profit – because property only goes up in value, yes?

We may have witnessed the greatest financial fraud of all time. Western societies have been guilty of living beyond their means, and the reckoning we face is a sobering jolt. As the cartoonist Walt Kelly put it: 'I have met the enemy, and he is us.'

Only risk-positive entrepreneurs have the guts to risk making fresh investments in this environment, a time when investment is exactly what society needs to pick itself up again.

Watch out for an epidemic of petty fraud

The economist J. K. Galbraith asserted that fraud rose in a bull market and shrank in a slump. As he put it, the 'bezzle' rises in a boom because of lax controls, and fades in a bust.

Colossal frauds like Bernard Madoff's Ponzi scheme suggests Galbraith may be right about large-scale embezzlement, but my experience is the opposite when it comes to petty larceny.

One of our restaurant companies suffered a disturbing rise in insurance claims. It wasn't down to carelessness. Several claims related to apparent falls by suppliers' workers. The curious thing is that in more than one case the victim appears to have waited more than fifteen months before notifying us of the injury.

After talking to other operators, it seems that during a downturn the hospitality trade suffers a plague of legal letters from claimants looking for free money. No doubt some are genuine; but others are trying it on, I am sure, because they are feeling the pinch, and think negligence claims are easy money.

Unfortunately, insurers often settle small claims even if they are doubtful, simply to save legal fees and administrative bother. But this policy of expediency only encourages others to try the same con.

Similarly, at another retail business I own I had trouble with several thefts of large sums of cash from branches, all carried out by insiders. In each case those responsible have been caught, but it is very depressing to have to deal with employee dishonesty. One feels a despairing sense of betrayal, especially if senior staff is involved. Too often all that happens to the perpetrators is that they lose their job, even if they are reported to the police.

As with all such lawless behaviour, these incidents can destroy trust in the workplace, and lead to unhealthy suspicion between owners and staff. The answer is to have thorough systems and checks and balances. But no method of prevention is perfect, and crooks are ingenious at inventing ways round what appears to be foolproof security.

Meanwhile, there's a rapid rise in 'friendly fraud'. These are cases in which online or mail-order customers falsely claim that goods were never sent, or recipients return the wrong items for a refund. The customer obtains a credit-card chargeback and the vendor is out of pocket.

Vigilance and a proportionate response are required of leaders. Perhaps the most important thing is to avoid slipping into a sense of paranoia, and maintain the belief that the vast majority of people are honest, whatever the conditions.

Time to go on the offensive

So what can you do when a recession eviscerates your top-line revenue? First of all, you cut costs like a dervish, just to stay solvent. But you cannot maintain that survival mentality for ever. At some point every organization has to progress or disintegrate.

In shrinking industries, for most businesses there is only one way to expand: take market share.

In the Darwinian world of capitalism, during downturns plenty of weaker operators cease trading or choose to sell up. The priority for the ambitious is to be on the other side of that transaction, and seize the failing concern's customers, or simply buy its assets.

Snapping up a small competitor can help to streamline affairs rapidly by using your production, accounting, IT, purchasing, training, HR and marketing resources across both operations. Such apparent bargains are rare, but they do come up occasionally.

These types of opportunity are the result of tumultuous circumstances. Badly managed, heavily indebted and structurally unsound companies will sadly fall by the wayside like victims of the plague. And while capital is scarce, the actual cost of this sort of deal is often modest compared with the price it would have commanded in boom times.

The deciding factors in making a success of such moves are the ability to move swiftly and having industrial logic on your side. You must be able to integrate any purchase and derive genuine synergies efficiently. This is not a forgiving climate if you overreach and under-deliver.

It takes bold vision to assume the additional risk of such manoeuvres in this ferocious storm. One may be too early – the downturn could get even bloodier. And there are plenty of entrepreneurs who have been so battered as to lose their nerve. But as General Foch said during the Battle of the Marne: 'Hard pressed to my right; my left is in retreat; my centre is yielding. Situation excellent. Attack!'

Recessions produce all sorts of forced sellers, distressed companies that have breached bank covenants or are chronically loss making, with exhausted or insolvent owners. Buildings, contracts, equipment, stock – all manner of assets can be had, in some instances for a pittance. This permits the winning players to exercise more pricing power, use operational gearing and squeeze economies of scale to deliver returns.

Not all such initiatives have to be acquisitions. They could be organic growth plans – product launches, new hires or major capital expenditure. There is abundant human talent available, and property galore. But you need a superior business model and an appetite for hard work to cope with the challenges. No one is saying it is easy: finding and executing the right corporate purchases is an art, and requires lots of luck. But it sure beats stagnation.

Hard times reveal the true opportunists

It should be clear by now that downturns are not by any means all bad. They are a necessary evil of the capitalist system. They clear out the excess. During booms there is misallocation of capital and wasteful spending. We all get complacent and overconfident.

'There is in the worst of fortune the best of chances for a happy change'

Euripides

Slumps help to ensure that resources are not squandered, but used productively. Organizations are forced to get fit or shut down.

Take personnel. During the good times it can be difficult to hire competent staff, and employers may even have to offer inducements to recruit. But when things get tough, talent becomes much more accessible as the jobs get scarcer. And existing workers try harder, knowing that if they get laid off they may not easily find another post.

Premises become much more widely available. I recall that from 1993 to 1995 we were rapidly able to expand PizzaExpress because of the wide availability of suitable restaurant sites at attractive rents. The recession eliminated competition and landlords were desperate for someone to occupy space.

Busts also force suppliers to price sensibly. During the dotcom bubble it was impossibly expensive to build a website. In 1999 we spent a full year's profits at Whittard of Chelsea, the tea and coffee retailer, on an online store – but most of the money was squandered. Three years later such services could be built for 10 per cent of what we spent. The huge expansion in e-commerce could not have happened without the ubiquity of better-value technology.

Recessions give policy makers more latitude. Negligible economic growth permits the authorities to cut interest rates. That helps stimulate the creation of credit. Inflation tends to fall if demand falters. A weak economy might even persuade the government to deregulate and reduce taxes to boost business activity.

Thus can opportunity arise from adversity. Plenty of great fortunes were founded in the depths of a recession. In the post-war austerity of London in 1948, Donald Gosling and Ronald Hobbs bought a bomb site in Red Lion Square, Holborn – and so began National Car Parks. They foresaw the expansion of car ownership and the consequent rise in demand for parking. They sold NCP in 1998 for £800 million. Not bad for an initial investment of just £200.

Losing your reputation

One of the great myths is that your reputation is your most precious asset, and that you can only lose it once.

In truth, throughout my business career I have met ex-bandits who have been rehabilitated and are now fêted. They might have been personally bankrupt, mismanaged bust companies or been thrown off boards for scurrilous behaviour. But provided someone has not been convicted of mass murder, it seems most things are forgivable.

The most straightforward way of repairing your reputation is to become very rich. It is extraordinary how large sums of money bring on bouts of amnesia in the grandest investment bankers, who would previously have been the harshest critics. Success works as a powerful magnet. For example, it was amazing how many supporters came out for billionaire Russian oligarch Mikhail Khodorkovsky when he was prosecuted

'Whatever
ignominy or
disgrace we
have incurred, it
is almost always
in our power to
re-establish our
reputation'

François de la Rochefoucauld

by Putin. How many overlooked his behaviour in the late 1990s towards creditors and minority shareholders in his company Yukos?

But then none of us are perfect, or indeed possess infallible judgment. Those who take risks are human and will sometimes fail. It goes with the territory. The most popular after-dinner speech I give is the recital of my worst mistakes and what I hope I've learned from them. I deliver it as a contrast to the endless boasting we hear from too many TV-star entrepreneurs. Invariably, those who have stumbled and then recovered are more rounded characters for the experience.

Apart from money, the other cure for 'financial difficulties' is time. The merry-go-round of commerce revolves swiftly, and after a few years most of the faces are new: fund managers, analysts, journalists, bank officers and so on. In bull markets greed will soon overcome those concerns about a slightly chequered history, and for the right proposition investors, lenders and cheerleaders will soon be queuing up.

My favourite corporate resurrection is that of William Durant. He was the heroic industrialist who founded General Motors in 1908. He built an automotive empire in just two years through thirty acquisitions. But the manic corporate activity led to losses, and the bankers forced him out. So he resigned and founded Chevrolet, which was sufficiently successful that six years later he was able to gain control of GM once more. He was a buccaneer who cut corners, but he still created in a few years what rapidly became the world's largest business. If capitalism becomes so bureaucratic and fearful that it cannot cope with free-wheeling adventurers who've screwed up a few times, then we are all doomed.

In my view energy, intelligence, good health and an enterprising outlook are more important than an apparently great reputation. I have met a number of legendary figures who come showered with recommendations. All too often they turn out to be disappointments, possessing little desire to actually work and prove themselves. And I have also met dozens of hugely impressive individuals who have endured nasty shocks early in their careers – but then recovered the trust of backers and eventually repaid that faith in spades.

I like George Bernard Shaw's remark: 'My reputation grows with every failure.' The vital thing is to keep grafting away, and ignore the critics and brickbats as far as you can. Talent, originality and persistence will usually get you to your preferred destination in the end, whatever your reputation.

Getting fired

Most of us have been fired at some time or another – but only a few admit it. The rest are in denial, or glossing over the truth to keep their CVs unblemished. We might have been sacked from a job, an account, a project, or by a client. But life continues, new opportunities arise.

I have been given the boot on more than one occasion, but the experience has only encouraged me to try harder. Steve Jobs said: 'Getting fired from Apple

'That which doesn't kill you makes you stronger'

Friedrich Nietzsche

was the best thing that could have happened to me.'
He went off and founded neXT, then Pixar, and then
returned to Apple, and made it vastly more successful
than it had ever been. For him, losing his role at the
company he founded was a stimulus to make a new
start.

I can empathize. As a stockbroking analyst in the
1980s I was passed over for promotion by my then
boss (who went on to become a chairman of insurance giant Prudential). I don't really blame him – I
was never cut out to be a bank employee. I left shortly
afterwards and took up entrepreneurial activities, and
have never regretted my move.

Earlier in my career I was axed when working as a
lab assistant at St Mary's Hospital in Paddington. In
truth I was glad to go: my task consisted of analysing
human excrement. There are occasions when losing a
job can be a relief.

Despite the fantasy of TV shows such as *The Ap-
prentice*, no one at a senior level is actually fired these
days. They invariably sign compromise agreements
while everyone keeps quiet and pretends nothing went
wrong. The alternative can be the grinding misery of
an employment tribunal: vast quantities of wasted
time, legal fees and – too often – outright lies. Meanwhile HR departments spend their lives dreaming
up euphemisms for dismissal: 'let go'; 'restructured';
'downsized'; 'discharged'; 'relieved of duties' – not
that anyone is fooled. Often the executioner says, 'It's
nothing personal' – but to the victim it's always personal. They can feel humiliated – but it can also lead to
an honest reappraisal.

On one occasion I turned down an investment after discovering why the proposed chief executive had left his previous job after just two years. He had been asked to go because of 'anger management' issues. Curiously this was not revealed in his business plan. Such omissions and reinterpretations of history are why employers now use specialists to verify résumés and references. Getting a new appointment wrong can be ferociously expensive, so employers are more careful than ever.

In truth, the hiring and sometimes the laying off of staff have always been realities in the private sector, and are necessary evils if our system is to keep functioning. Companies rise and fall, and the fortunes of their workers ride with that economic roller coaster. Mass redundancies can seem very unfair to those who are given the chop, but in a corporate rescue the alternative can be complete liquidation, with the whole organization shutting down and the entire workforce being thrown on the street.

Ultimately, unproductive jobs don't last: they just lead to more pain later on. Intelligent citizens know real jobs are not natural phenomena invented for the general benefit of society. Jobs are a by-product of someone's urge to build a business and create wealth for themselves.

Jobs for life are a trap anyway. To learn and experience all the world has to offer, it makes sense to change jobs at intervals, and consider switching careers if things turn bad. Otherwise you become stale and taken for granted. There are endless new vocations for those with get-up-and-go. More and more people are becoming contractors or self-employed anyway, for the freedom it offers. And perhaps the best thing about working for yourself is that no one can fire you.

I have an acquaintance whose transport empire was reduced to rubble by economic downturn. Twenty years of work turned to dust in a matter of months. His firm was made bankrupt; collapsing demand and soaring costs did for it. So now he sits at home in his leather armchair, hitting the vodka by eleven in the morning, mired in boredom, self-pity and regret. Endless days with nothing to do stretch in front of him like a desert of despair. His existence has gone from one of frantic activity to complete emptiness – no money, no confidence, and no energy.

Of course, losing a business is not usually a matter of actual life or death, but for a founder it can feel like a bereavement. Often their self-belief and career never recover. Each ruin can be a minor tragedy, littered with collateral damage to family, staff, suppliers and the like.

Should we feel pity for a defeated entrepreneur? Not really – there are more deserving victims all around. After all, business without the chance of failure is like heaven without hell: somehow the concept doesn't work.

Every business founder knows that their enterprise might one day be shut down. Those who speculate to accumulate must understand the consequences of losing. But few dwell on this possibility, otherwise the fear would defenestrate them. By nature they believe in an optimistic future, so caution and risk avoidance

'It is not from the benevolence of the butcher, the brewer, or the baker that we expect our dinner, but from their regard to their own interest. We address ourselves, not to their humanity, but to their self-love, and never talk to them of our own necessities, but of their advantages'

Adam Smith

are not part of their psychological make-up. They are competitive to the core, and winning is the only option.

A handful of entrepreneurs were astute or lucky enough to cash out before the music stopped. Characters like Jon Hunt of Foxtons estate agents, and David Wilson of house builders Wilson Bowden, were wise enough to see that the boom times could not last for ever, and took cash off the table when it was available. They were sufficiently pragmatic to stifle any emotional urge to hold on to their creation, and swapped it for liquidity. They knew that even great businesses can peak, and that in commerce, as in everything, timing is all.

It isn't easy being a corporate cheerleader when the economy is having a heart attack. Yet there is no choice but to soldier on, focusing on short-term survival, so that one is still standing when the recovery eventually takes hold. All the time the dreadful mechanics of operational gearing in reverse apply: for every 15 per cent off the top line, the bottom line falls 50 per cent or more.

Downsizing is never fun: the unpleasant choices about what and who to cut are dehumanizing. Meanwhile, motivating staff can be a titanic challenge if they are afraid for their jobs, and see their bonuses stripped away, their overtime cancelled.

It requires real strength of character and courage to captain the ship during such turmoil. And persuading a nervous bank to stay supportive takes a rare and delicate mixture of charm and steel.

I recommend you try to stay healthy by taking

exercise to release endorphins and relieve stress. And avoid the media, because its relentless barrage of grim news can only dispirit anyone trying to hold the tide.

A philosopher friend of mine suggested the meditations of Marcus Aurelius to help put economic turbulence into perspective. Aurelius was Roman emperor during periods of plague, famine and war, before his wife's death and his subsequent prolonged exile from Rome while fending off hordes of barbarians.

Through it all, he retained a stoic outlook, and his writing reminds us just how lucky most of us are, and just how much of our mental state in troubled times is in our own hands. He wrote, 'Take away the complaint "I have been harmed", and the harm is taken away.'

Part 7
THE ENTREPRENEUR AT LARGE

Inventors are heroes

Society has a curious attitude towards inventors. Their brilliance over the centuries touches all of our lives in countless ways, yet we mostly take their efforts for granted. Indeed, more often than not in Britain we caricature them as eccentric boffins, like Caractacus Potts in *Chitty Chitty Bang Bang*. This ambivalence is a mistake; to me, they are perhaps the greatest heroes of all.

It is a great shame that so much innovation now seems to stem from nameless teams inside large corporations. The whole idea of technological progress had so much more personality in the era of giants like Nikola Tesla and Thomas Edison. There are too few such inspirational figures around today to dazzle and excite. Perhaps the solitary ideas of one person are not enough to produce real technological progress in the twenty-first century.

Yet the spirit of independent innovation springs eternal. I can recommend the 2008 movie *Flash of Genius*, based on an article (also now a book) by John Seabrook. It tells the true story of Bob Kearns, the professor who pioneered the intermittent windscreen wiper for cars. He showed it to the Ford Motor Company in 1969, but subsequently entered into interminable litigation with it, almost reminiscent of Jarndyce and Jarndyce in Charles Dickens's *Bleak House*. More than twenty years later, he settled for $10.2 million, but only after legal action had taken over his life.

Unfortunately, patent infringement is a fact of life

for inventors. Sir James Dyson, inventor of the bagless vacuum cleaner, talks in his autobiography *Against The Odds* (Orion, 1997) about various lawsuits against both Hoover and Amway. Knowledge of patent law and persistence bordering on the obsessive seem useful attributes if you want to be a successful inventor.

The subject of intellectual property and its protection is a contentious one. Many industries, such as the pharmaceutical trade, can only exist thanks to laws that allow them to enjoy temporary monopolies for original products. Vast, long-term research and development expenditure can only be recouped because of this complex system.

But some would argue that charging high prices (which often bear no relation to the cost of production) for life-saving drugs is immoral. Certainly, the juicy profits enjoyed by big pharma in the US are part of the reason that health-care costs there are so high – yet we are all beneficiaries of their discoveries and formulations.

I believe in freedom for enterprise, but I also think entrepreneurs must be allowed to reap the just rewards for their efforts. Moreover, it is clear that some abuse the patent system to prevent progress. Too many patents are now issued, many of dubious merit – especially in the field of software patents. Patent trolls abound – those who file 'paper patents' or 'submarine patents' that they never intend to exploit, but merely use as tools to sue unwitting infringers. Both Research in Motion, maker of the BlackBerry, and even Microsoft have suffered from this harmful toll on endeavour.

Inventors I have met are fundamentally motivated by a desire to see their creations become appreciated and recognized, rather than an urge to accumulate wealth. Tim Berners-Lee, the man responsible more than any other for the initiation of the world wide web, is a classic example of this attitude. He is a modest academic who has, I am sure, resisted countless overtures to make huge fortunes from the web, in order to carry on his role as one of its custodians.

Some inventors are almost dismissive of accountants and bankers – they say the money men do not understand the way creative minds work. Yet inventors must have a deeply practical streak: they need to think of ways to fabricate new things. The best inventors are a combination of artist and engineer: they have the vision to imagine a new device and the ability to make it come to life.

We need inventors more than ever if we are to improve the world. From a cure for Alzheimer's to better car batteries, there are thousands of urgent problems that need solving.

History suggests the magical combination of technology, capitalism and the spirit of invention is, despite the doubts of the pessimists, capable of meeting every challenge.

Every struggling entrepreneur inventor can take comfort from the noble lineage to which they belong.

Women inventors

Why do men make over 95 per cent of all patent applications? Are they better at taking risks? Do they have more technical, practical minds? Or are there cultural barriers that discourage women from becoming inventors?

Those who introduce new ideas often have to confront the old order of things and challenge convention. Historically men were usually in a better position to do that, and their exploring and hunting instincts perhaps help them in the quest for original devices. But women are frequently more organized and efficient than men, and invention demands a systematic approach to discovery. And so it should come as no surprise that essential breakthroughs have been pioneered by women, despite many deterrents put in their way. Their stories serve as inspiration for any entrepreneur.

Astoundingly, the first business computer software program was devised by a woman. Grace Hopper trained as a mathematician and was working at Sperry Corporation when she developed COBOL, a compiler language still in use today. Throughout her life she broke barriers inhibiting women's progress in the workplace. She ended her career when she retired from the US Navy as a rear admiral in 1985 aged seventy-nine – the oldest person on active duty.

Possibly the most impressive female scientist of modern times was Dr Gertrude Elion, following in the footsteps of the French genius Marie Curie. Elion spent over twenty-five years in the pharmaceutical business researching for Burroughs-Wellcome. During that time she developed Purinethol, the first drug to treat leukaemia, and Imuran, which prevents the rejection of transplant organs. Later her team synthesized acyclovir, the anti-herpes drug better known as Zovirax. During her productive career she received forty-five patents, ten honorary doctorates and the Nobel Prize in Medicine in 1988.

Another successful female industrial scientist was Patsy Sherman. She worked for 3M Corporation and together with a colleague invented the Scotchgard fabric-protection process. Like so many discoveries, this was stumbled upon by accident – someone in the lab spilled a new compound on their tennis shoes and they found water couldn't penetrate the material. It took seven years of trial and error before a commercial product was born – which is still the brand leader today.

Inevitably, a woman invented the bra. The pioneer was an aristocratic New Yorker called Polly Jacob. She patented a 'backless brassiere' in 1914. It was a simple undergarment constructed from two silk handkerchiefs and a length of pink ribbon. Unfortunately she found the rag trade hard work and sold her rights to the Warner Corset Company for $1,500. Ida Rosenthal, who together with her husband William founded the Maiden Form Brassiere Company in 1923 with $4,500, invented a garment rather more like today's bra. The company continues in business to this day and remains a major force in the underwear trade.

Unsurprisingly, a woman secretary invented

correction fluid for typists. Bette Nesmith, a divorced single mother, got fed up with retyping whole letters in her job at a Dallas bank. So in 1951 she prepared a bottle of white paint to erase typing errors. Eventually she named her product Liquid Paper and turned it into a business. The business grew steadily over the next few decades until she sold out to Gillette in 1979. And while Bette was building her office-products empire, her son Mike went on to become one of the Monkees pop group.

The list of ingenious women inventors goes on. In 1903 Mary Anderson filed a patent for the world's first windscreen wiper, more or less unchanged until Bob Kearns's design improvements in the 1960s. It was designed to fit on trams so that drivers could mechanically remove snow to enable them to see properly. And in 1951 Marion Donovan patented the disposable nappy, or 'Boater' as she nicknamed her prototype. She eventually sold her business for $1 million and proceeded to pioneer other inventions.

These women belie the unhelpful stereotype of the inventor as an eccentric, an absent-minded male boffin. Entrepreneurialism is a broad church, one that cares little for culturally received notions.

Innovation and reality

Life is a collision of reality and dreams. And while great dreams are important, reality is even more so.

In my perfect world I would have been a famous

inventor, like Thomas Alva Edison. To have introduced to the world the phonograph and light bulb, among many other advances, is a magnificent achievement. The sort of thing I do is far more derivative, even if I enjoy it and am proud of it.

But Edison was not only imaginative; he was also prolific and industrious. He was at heart a practical man grounded in reality, an essential trait if new products are to be commercial. Edison said: 'The three great essentials to achieve anything worthwhile are first, hard work; second, stick-to-itiveness; third, common sense.' His down-to-earth attitude is a reminder that ideas alone are worthless – what is needed is application.

It's clear that expedience is vital for the entrepreneur inventor, as the story of air conditioning serves to show. As an invention, air conditioning is perhaps as important an advance as any over the last century or so. In 1902, Dr Willis Carrier, an engineer recently out of Cornell University earning just $10 a week, invented a mechanism he called process cooling, for use in a printing plant in Brooklyn. Reputedly he had his brainwave while waiting for his train on a cold, foggy night. He patented his 'Apparatus for Testing Air' four years later – and kick-started an entire industry. Carrier employed a centrifugal system that used the evaporation of a refrigerant liquid to cool and dehumidify the environment.

Carrier was a classic American man of action. He said: 'I fish only for edible fish, and hunt only for edible game, even in the laboratory.' Remarkably, the business he founded remains the world leader today, a division of United Technologies Corporation with annual sales of $11 billion. Not bad for a business incorporated in 1915 with capital of just $35,000.

Expedience has always been my watchword in the restaurant industry – restaurants are a wonderful showcase for the uses and abuses of runaway innovation. I am forever receiving business plans for a new dining-out concept from people who do not grasp that a novel restaurant formula is easy to devise.

The real challenge is execution – and persistence. Restaurant start-ups have a very high failure rate and so I have tended to back proven projects, investing fairly early on before they get too popular and expensive.

My partners and I took control of PizzaExpress at a time when the company was well established but owned only twelve sites with some franchises. We then expanded the business vigorously, exploiting a fantastic formula and rolling out the chain to 250 sites in my seven years as chairman.

We were lucky in that our timing was good: Peter Boizot, the brilliant founder, had fallen out with his partners and the firm needed fresh blood and capital. By the time we completed the deal Britain was coming out of recession but sites were plentiful and there was pent-up demand from the public to eat out in better surroundings and sample a much better product than the competition could provide.

It might seem that the restaurant industry is not a natural home for the innovative entrepreneur, but I have known several ingenious restaurant pioneers. In addition to Peter Boizot there is Alan Yau (Wagamama), Denis Blais (Belgo) and the late Bob Payton (My

Kinda Town), who launched the Chicago Rib Shack and Henry J. Beans.

Each is (or was) an original thinker, but men such as these are easily bored. After opening a few branches of a particular brand they become distracted and look for other things to do. In the case of Belgo and My Kinda Town, my partners and I took control of their fledgling empires and grew them simply by replicating their work. They had made mistakes, corrected them, and reduced the chance of failure. Their offerings were already popular – they just needed commercializing fully.

I started Strada from scratch. My experience with PizzaExpress told me there was plenty of profit in pizza and Italian cuisine. So we gave Strada a more authentic feel than PizzaExpress, with wood-fired ovens, larger, thin-crust pizza and a broader menu that included pasta, risotto, and grilled meat and fish dishes. Prices were slightly higher and ingredients better quality, and kitchen staff rather better trained.

Our first outlet in Battersea didn't work, but we persevered. I followed the advice of Ray Kroc, billionaire creator of the McDonald's empire, the world's largest restaurant chain, who said: 'Press on. Nothing in the world can take the place of persistence.' We kept going and then Strada started working: today there are over fifty of them throughout the UK.

These days I am chairman and part-owner of a restaurant business called Giraffe. My partner there is a veteran restaurateur called Russel Joffe, who earlier in his career founded Café Flo.

Giraffe is a great example of the Japanese philosophy

of *kaizen* mentioned earlier. For each new branch we consider different design possibilities; we constantly ask ourselves if we can do it better; we introduce new menus regularly; we are restless and never satisfied. Giraffe innovates by gradual but constant evolution, with lots of small alterations over time ultimately generating wholesale change.

This ability to question and adapt as conditions change and new competitors arrive is a characteristic of many sound firms. Channel 4, for example, has various features that allow it to innovate in its television more than some.

Firstly, from its founding, the organization has encouraged staff to join for a few years, give some of their best ideas, and then go off and work elsewhere – be it for a rival broadcaster or a production company. This turnover of talent is seen as a good thing. It is no coincidence that both the BBC and ITV have fielded chief executives who are ex-Channel 4 CEOs.

Secondly, Channel 4 is a commissioner: it relies on independent companies to make its programmes, using several hundred suppliers every year – big and small – to come up with breakthrough shows that will catch the imagination of the audience. All those external brains work on Channel 4's behalf to come up with television that is startling, unusual and groundbreaking.

Because the business world has so many entrenched interests, it's clear that innovation goes hand-in-hand with risk. What I enjoy about business is being occasioned to take risks. All capitalists are in the business of measured risk-taking. It's about

'Don't play for safety. It's the most dangerous game in the world'

Sir Hugh Walpole

accepting that something might not work, but giving it a go anyhow. You should not avoid bold decisions or challenging the orthodox. Be original and daring where it makes sense: you will gain the applause if it works, and even if you're wrong, at least you made an attempt.

We all cling to the illusion of certainty in life. We find it comforting to believe things are infallible. Modern technology underpins our faith in an error-free society. Yet at heart we know such stuff is nonsense. The universe is random and unpredictable, and those who try to eliminate the unexpected are doomed to an existence of anxiety and over-caution – and stifled creativity, no doubt. I like the reported maxim of Jong-Yong Jun, the former CEO of super-successful South Korean conglomerate Samsung Electronics: 'a culture of perpetual crisis'.

One of the diseases that grips institutions is the 'safety in numbers' philosophy – in other words, neurotic risk avoidance at all costs. This is the belief that as long as you follow the crowd – even if they're quite wrong – you can't be criticized for your work. Company boards and committees can make astounding errors thanks to peer pressure and the desire to conform – look at Northern Rock or Bear Stearns. Yet as General MacArthur said, 'There is no security on this earth. Only opportunity.'

I have studied the careers of a number of great entrepreneurs, and all of them followed Franklin D. Roosevelt's belief in 'bold, persistent experimentation'. And good old Thomas Edison again, while on his way to doing things like founding General Electric, said, 'I have not failed. I have just found 10,000 ways that won't work.'

After all, the worst that can happen if we make a wrong product decision is that we will lose money and waste time. There are worse things than that.

A while ago I went to Zimbabwe. In Harare I met a schoolteacher called Henry who spent much of his time covertly photographing and recording atrocities being committed by President Mugabe's thuggish followers. He took grave risks in the hope that his evidence might help bring about political improvement in that tragic country. About a month after I met him, Henry was set upon by Mugabe's Green Bombers and his leg was broken. But I hear he remains committed to the cause of freedom, and has not given up.

His actions exemplify Thornton Wilder's words: 'I know that every good and excellent thing in the world stands moment by moment on the razor-edge of danger and must be fought for.' That Zimbabwean schoolteacher – he's taking risks; the rest of us are just playing.

People in contemporary Western societies have become much less familiar with pain, loss, suffering and death than in previous ages. We actually enjoy unprecedented levels of comfort, good health and prosperity. Economists, politicians and the media make dark predictions about the decline of the West, environmental crisis, and so on. But these dangers are often more theoretical than real.

Right now the digital revolution has thrown many comfortable assumptions up in the air, and entire industries have been hurled into a period of violent change and uncertainty. But while such phases produce challenges, they all provide excitement for those with ambition, meat for those with hunger and fire in their belly.

We should never let temporary conditions blind us to the wonderful opportunities that always await those willing to try. Good old Teddy Roosevelt, one of my favourite American presidents, put it best: 'Far better it is to dare mighty things, to win glorious triumphs, even though chequered by failure, than to rank with those poor spirits who neither enjoy much nor suffer much, because they live in a grey twilight that knows not victory nor defeat.'

To those entrepreneurs who would take a risk on an innovative new product:

O be practical – execution is more important than theoretical ideas

O involve youth where you can – the young are more willing to change than their elders

O understand risk and embrace it where it makes sense, rather than seeing it as a sheer negative

O allow external influences

O be restless and *never* complacent.

I will end with a story told by John F. Kennedy. A great elderly French general once asked his gardener to plant a tree. The gardener objected that the tree was slow growing and would not reach maturity for a hundred years. The general replied: 'In that case, there is no time to be lost. Plant the tree this afternoon.'

All part of a good education

The part-time and temporary jobs I had while growing up were a vital part of my education. There was an authenticity about them that sitting in a classroom entirely lacked. They helped to teach me the importance of a work ethic, independence, and just how tough many real workplaces are. I worry that too few twenty-first-century teenagers get this type of experience – and that they are less well-rounded as a consequence.

I can recall sitting in the bath after my first day's work one Easter holiday in the late 1970s. The job was in a small engineering workshop. My task was to turn metal rods on a lathe all day. By 5 p.m. on my first day my hands were blistered and raw.

Although I went to a state school, I enjoyed a comfortable upbringing and had never experienced a proper labouring job. But at the end of the week I got my pay in cash in a brown envelope with a cellophane window. It was about £40. Earning all that through my own efforts was hugely satisfying. It made me feel almost rich, and grown up.

Every Christmas I used to work as a temporary postman in my village, helping to deliver the seasonal avalanche of parcels and greeting cards. This was before the Internet and mobile phones, so the Royal Mail was a much more important way to keep in touch than it is now. You had to start very early, but you generally finished your round by lunchtime. The worst aspect was rain. If it was wet, you still had to finish the task, even if it took four hours. You ended up soaked, and the letters were hardly dry either. I remember being tempted to chuck a lot of post away on one day, but was reminded that doing so was a very serious offence. I think of postmen struggling in the rain every time I drive by the splendid Eighth Avenue general post office in Manhattan, and see the evocative inscription, which reads: 'Neither snow nor rain nor heat nor gloom of night stays these couriers from the swift completion of their appointed rounds.'

I realized that finding something to do that you love from Monday to Friday was a vital ingredient to a fulfilling life. It became a mission of mine to pursue obsessively a livelihood where I could look forward to Monday morning rather than dread it.

As a first-year undergraduate studying medicine, I worked at St Mary's Hospital in London for an eminent professor during the vacation. He was studying the connection between cardiovascular disease and extended use of the contraceptive pill. I was a lab assistant – this was the human-excrement job I mentioned – and my boss was something of a tyrant. It helped put me off medicine as a vocation, and indeed working for other people.

At university I worked as a DJ for a mobile discotheque, spinning the discs at everything from student gigs to weddings. Once I gained confidence, I acquired my own turntables and loved the combination of working hard, playing music, meeting girls and earning money. I realized that being an entrepreneur was the answer – you could control your own destiny and

you received the rewards for your efforts. With partners I ran weekly dances at a local nightclub. It made
money from the start, and I saw that running a business could give you enormous freedom and creative
stimulation.

For me, holiday and student jobs provided lessons
in life and an insight that academic, formal education
could never match. I wonder how many children of
the readers of this book will have paying jobs while
studying? Not enough, I fear.

The reputation of business

I spend most of my time working in the private equity
industry. It is subject to regular criticism over its activities. It joins sectors like the food business and the
pharmaceutical trade, which have suffered from negative scrutiny for some time. But are these attacks on
their reputations fair or constructive?

Business doesn't do a great job at explaining what
it contributes to society. Traditional economics bores
most people. More should be done with think tanks,
lobbyists, public relations and academic research to
explain how our entire way of life depends upon business to provide us with the goods and services we use
every day. The various trade organizations do their
bit, but they fail to capture the public's imagination or
stimulate excitement about the extraordinary benefit
that capitalism brings to everyone.

Surveys show most citizens are suspicious of big

business. Yet the private sector pays all the taxes, provides all the wealth-generating jobs, and keeps the entire system going. Industry needs to invest more in its public image. Without business everything we rely on would collapse.

Too many opinion formers have a naive view that the public sector is somehow morally superior to the private sector – that the profit motive is a grubby urge. After all, companies have to justify themselves every day in the marketplace. They rely on repeat purchases. If customers feel ripped off or lied to, they stop buying – and the company goes bust. If private equity houses, drugs companies, television stations and food manufacturers were so terrible, then eventually the public would shun them all, because in a free market there is always a choice.

But with the state, there is almost no choice. You cannot change your tax department or planning authority if you feel like it. In most countries only a handful of parties stand any chance of assuming government, and they only stand for election every few years. In the meantime politicians vote in line with their party to retain their seats, salaries, expenses and pensions. They enjoy the status and power, and see it as their divine duty to pass more laws. But this endless, stifling outpouring of legislation only inhibits enterprise and progress.

Advances in technology and entrepreneurial ingenuity mean more and better things are available than ever before, despite the welter of unnecessary regulation. The quality and range of food in our supermarkets is astounding: the idea this cornucopia is less healthy than in the past is preposterous. Similarly, the notion that twenty-five years ago television was generally better – something I'd occasionally hear when I worked in the industry – is tosh. Take a look at a schedule from then and see how many repeats and unwatchable rubbish was being shown, and what limited choice there was.

Fundamentally, business believes in the future and needs an optimistic frame of mind.

Investment and fertile invention come only from those who relish progress. Entrepreneurs know that, by most measures, life is improving, but the liberal news media and unions are different. They thrive on conflict and the idea of things getting worse. They believe they expose the truth, and their role is to stop the robber barons of business from wrecking our green and pleasant land and exploiting the downtrodden workers. The business community needs to take these critics seriously, and engage assertively with policy makers and activists. Every business figurehead should stand up and act as an advocate in a long-term campaign to educate the public about the real source of our prosperity.

What's so terrible about making money?

One thing that has always baffled me is why certain people hate capitalism so much. They really are missing something.

Ever since I was eighteen and co-founded a business by accident, I knew that being an entrepreneur was the most fun you could have with your clothes on – it is the greatest adventure modern life has to offer. And if you're lucky and hard working, you might even get rich in the process. Why is that so terrible? Yet all too often capitalism is blamed for many of the ills of modern life, from global warming to poverty.

I remain convinced that many intelligent, ambitious individuals would adopt a self-employed way of life if they could strip away all the cultural bias and realize that building a venture can be a creative endeavour – heroic, even.

Entrepreneurship is a vocation, like fine art or quantum physics or teaching. But intellectual snobbery, prejudice and the comfort blanket of big organizations mean capitalism frequently fails to win the moral arguments.

Plenty of opinion-formers in places like Brussels and Whitehall too often think the world is a zero-sum place: they believe that each commercial success is bought at the cost of someone else's failure. Anti-capitalists suggest that the solution to inequality is re-distribution – which actually means levelling down.

Churchill understood this malaise when he said: 'The inherent vice of capitalism is the unequal sharing of the blessings. The inherent blessing of socialism is the equal sharing of misery.'

Central planners forget how the inventive instinct is stimulated and assume the worst of markets. Such intervention can carry a high price: the catastrophic unintended consequences of biofuel mania spring to mind. Will the high-minded political classes admit the error of the biofuel argument and swiftly abandon the mad incentives that are contributing to food riots and encouraging deforestation? I doubt it.

One of the wonderful things about markets is that they self-correct ruthlessly: companies that fail to serve the customer will be overwhelmed by rivals – and go bust – and see their assets reallocated. But governments move slowly, ideologues can be stubborn and damaging legislation can take years to rescind.

Most people focus on the risks of free enterprise and are scared to join the ranks of the self-made. Some have learned to play the system of government and institutions like a game, and enjoy power, pension and profit from their position in the state sector. Why should they encourage choice and competition when they have such a safe haven as a bureaucrat, trade union official or academic?

I hope by the very fact that you have bought this book that you are either already in business for yourself, or planning to be. Your country needs you!

Stress and risk: the secrets of happiness

I once participated in a debate entitled 'The good society: virtues for a post-recession world'. A couple of my fellow panellists emphasized the importance of promoting happiness rather than material wealth as a true measure of human progress. They believe that advances in gross domestic product are an inferior way to achieve greater well-being, and that a concept such as 'gross national happiness' might be a better tool. As I listened to their definitions of happiness, I realized that not many coincided with my view of what made entrepreneurs tick.

There is no stereotypical entrepreneurial personality, but one can identify characteristics that most entrepreneurs share. At heart they are highly competitive. They do not seek security as their main goal – rather, they actively seek risk, and enjoy overcoming stressful challenges. They are not sheer gamblers, but they embrace dynamism and, to have the chance to win, they are willing to invest in spite of the possibility of failure.

For many other people a contented existence might be summed up in Max Ehrmann's poem 'Desiderata', which more or less defines the opposite of the entrepreneurial life: 'Go placidly amid the noise and haste . . . Exercise caution in your business affairs' . . . and so on. By contrast, entrepreneurs are in a hurry: they stir things up and disrupt; they overturn companies and ways of doing business; they invent better products and threaten the status quo; they relish upheaval because it presents opportunities to supplant the existing order.

All this innovation and change is in stark contrast to the view espoused by many philosophers and writers, namely that happiness means stability and tranquillity. To a restless, striving entrepreneur those calm objectives represent boredom.

Perhaps a relaxed life is the right answer for some, but to me it would be deadly dull. Where is the stimulation in a safe career? I have rarely opted for the easy path if the alternative offered the possibility of something with more fireworks. To me, achieving something novel and bold is meaningful, and practising meditation isn't.

The economist Richard Layard, who puts himself forward as an authority on happiness, says public policy should demotivate wealth creators with higher taxation, because they exacerbate the race for status. But he also says we must eliminate high unemployment. And I suspect that these two objectives are intrinsically incompatible. Entrepreneurs, for all their rivalry and dissent, are the principal engines that can create jobs. Discouraging them will only make the problem of unemployment worse.

A society is condemned to stagnate if it rejects material advancement, takes a degraded view of humankind as an exploiter and adopts a fatalistic perspective of our system. Why would a world of deliberately diminished expectations lead to increased contentment? I worry that politicians will use the promise of upgrading our overall 'quality of life' as a false flag in order to pursue more government intrusion, greater regulation and higher levels of redistribution.

Happiness is about independence and freedom, and vital engagement with one's craft in a productive way. I have faith in humanity, and applaud those who attempt to improve their lot. For millions, this involves something of a heroic daily struggle. Inevitably, that is unlikely to lead to a peaceful existence, but why should we meekly accept drudgery and disadvantage?

A parlour game for the highly motivated

A clever entrepreneur I know has a favourite parlour game; it works best if the participants are decidedly ambitious. He asks them to choose their personal ranking for the three primal motivations, namely money, power and recognition. Do they value money over power and recognition? The player must list all three in descending order. Their answer tells them which career steps to take.

The quiz encapsulates the vital drivers in a blunt but brilliant way. It cuts out the fluff. The ingenuity of the selection is the simplicity: it boils down lots of complicated psychometric testing to three factors. And I like the honesty of the words. Unlike so many questionnaires, it does not pretend that our desires are all worthy. It asks us if we are, in the darkest parts of our souls, predominantly avaricious, megalomaniac or conceited.

Some respondents attempt to flout the rules by selecting some fourth option for their overriding motive, such as an urge to 'do good' or some similar affectation. But this contest is too ruthless for such stuff. It acknowledges that gentle souls, who really believe in noble causes above all else, are unlikely to rise to the top in business, politics, the media and so forth. Kind folk spend their lives working with the underprivileged or the equivalent, and I suspect that they do not meet people like my friend.

Many would assume that entrepreneurs will always plump for 'money' first on their list. In the early years of struggle to achieve some sort of breakthrough, that is probably right. Moreover, measuring the score is much easier with money than power or recognition.

But my experience is that the self-employed will very often rank 'recognition' first – especially if they have already made a bit of capital. They have worked out that an extra million or two is not likely to change their lives, but that media attention or a role in a political party, for example, will add an extra dimension to their existence.

Indeed, I suspect that many corporate executives probably rank money at least second. They are not likely to amass the riches that a private business owner can enjoy. But they might command a giant empire, and enjoy the fame of running a huge public company. Almost all very large enterprises are public companies, or institutionally owned. Anyone who fights their way to the summit of that sort of organization must want to possess power.

I think the game also identifies the ever-present dividing line between those who ply their trade in the private sector and those who work in the public or non-profit world. For the entrepreneur, money will be first or second; for those in the state sector it will surely be last. This reveals the materialism at the heart of every wealth-creator. But is that worse than the urge to control that so stimulates those who run the police, universities, hospitals, schools, government and army?

At a recent dinner party I sat next to a fairly senior politician. I asked him the power/money/recognition question, and he unhesitatingly put 'power' in first place. I admired his straight talking, but wondered about the psychology of someone so compelled to take charge of others' lives.

Of course, our behaviour is determined by more than just these three base cravings. The will to create, for instance, is an enormous element of every artist's life – and for many business builders too. The pride of invention, of craftsmanship, the satisfaction of originating something – I believe that sensation transcends the parlour game categories. But it is very rarely enough. Usually, it is intermingled with a lust for status, wealth or influence, or perhaps all three.

Is this a game with winners and losers? Superficially, no: it is about self-examination. Yet I think the way the player conducts the game is what matters. People who are ashamed of what they want will fudge their answers, but those who can answer with a confident and realistic air will surely seem the victor.

Satisfying the soul

'I don't think that business ever satisfies the soul.' That remark was made by Sir Robin Saxby just after he retired as chairman of ARM, the highly successful technology company. He is an intelligent man who built a pioneering, world-class operation – and yet he appears to find his major career achievements unfulfilling. Why?

It might be that Sir Robin is a restless man who would never find work truly enriching, whatever his job was. Or it might be that business appears to him to be too down-to-earth to be intellectually stimulating, compared with more artistic or seemingly altruistic pursuits like writing, teaching or research. But perhaps business generally does a poor job of justifying itself, and reminding everyone of its profound contribution to each aspect of our entire way of life – and perhaps business leaders are not proud enough of what they do.

I wholeheartedly disagree with the view that business cannot satisfy the soul. I think it offers many of the essential ingredients for a fruitful life.

Firstly, it is all about freedom. Starting and running an enterprise is the best way of controlling your own destiny and perhaps changing the world. I believe it is a very basic instinct from early childhood to want to make an impact on one's surroundings, to make a positive difference to society. Creating an enterprise is perhaps the most effective way of doing that ever devised. What can be more important than actually creating jobs? Essentially new business is about upsetting the status quo, thereby leading to progress. I think that is a virtuous mission.

Business is a fantastic technique for someone from a modest background, with minimal education, to improve their life and get ahead. Entrepreneurs often have few qualifications and would have been unable to enter more 'noble' professions such as politics, law or academia. Perhaps that is why so many of the intellectual elite have always looked down on those in trade and industry. They resent the fact that in the capitalist system, uneducated but energetic individuals can reach positions of power and wealth through sheer effort.

Perhaps it is the profit motive that offends the spiritual. But profit is the essential lubricant that enables mankind to advance. Inefficient and loss-making firms die, and can cause havoc for owners, staff and customers. But productive firms tend to create a virtuous circle: they do well, attract talent, pay more, make investors good returns, and can afford to launch better products. This is called progress.

Presently there are all too many sceptics who think capitalism and consumerism are destroying the planet, thanks to global warming and so forth. These doubters underestimate the inventive ability of entrepreneurs to find solutions to these apparent problems. They also propose a sort of apartheid, by denying the developing world our standard of living.

Another reason I like business is because it is realistic. Too much focus on the inner self and contemplation of the meaning of life can lead to a melancholy existence. Business involves engaging with the world

– it is about action, not vague concepts. The last sentence in Richard Schoch's *The Secrets of Happiness* (Profile, 2006) rings true to me: 'Our life is ever striving, and we call that striving happiness.' Business is all about striving for a better future – not just dreaming.

Business is also humanitarian. It has reduced child mortality and brought about increased life expectancy and countless other advances in material welfare. Industrial capitalism has replaced political systems so much worse that there is no moral comparison. It thrives in democracies where there is rule of law, free trade and property rights. In totalitarian regimes – on both the left and right – free enterprise withers. In particular, the bloodiest regimes in history – responsible for perhaps 50 million deaths – were the virulently anti-business, communist states of Russia and China during the twentieth century.

It is true that too much time in business is absorbed by bureaucrats, lawyers, administration and suchlike. But the essence of business is the creative breakthrough, the new discovery, the fantastic new product launch, the wildly successful start-up. The former processes are necessary for the latter to work.

But the secret to finding fulfilment – in business, in life – is to retain a vital engagement in the drama of it all.

Acknowledgements

I would like to pay special thanks to my advisor Jason Dunne, who helped every step of the way in the researching, writing and editing of this book. I would also like to thank Ravi Mattu and Lionel Barber at the *Financial Times*, who have encouraged my writing over the years, and before them Neil Bennett, who first took a gamble with me at the *Sunday Telegraph*. My assistant Helen Carnie provided dedicated support for this book and all areas of my work. I am grateful to Joel Rickett for commissioning this book and working with me to ensure its eventual publication, and also Trevor Horwood for doing a first-class job of copy-editing the text. I am also thankful to my partners at Risk Capital, especially Ben Redmond, for indulging me while I take time away from our core business to write. And of course the biggest thanks go to my wonderful wife Liza, for being the best partner anyone could ever want.